Praise for
The Secret Handshake

"*The Secret Handshake,* Kathleen Reardon's new and most important book, takes 'organizational politics' out of the closet and illuminates the darkness surrounding that topic. It is an extremely original, brave, and useful book about the social etiquette of modern bureaucracies—i.e., how to get things done through people. And it's a topic that, if discussed at all, is usually spoken about in dark and uninformed ways. Reardon not only clarifies the topic but shows convincingly that unless one has an enlightened view of what organizational politics is all about, one is doomed to failure."

—Warren Bennis, Distinguished Professor of Business Administration at USC and author of *Managing the Dream*

"*The Secret Handshake* delivers powerful insights into the real calculus of corporate decision-making. It not only sheds light on the poorly understood pinnacles of power, but provides a primer for those who would play the game."

—Bill Da~~vi~~ ~~ion~~ ~~ESA Research,~~
~~an~~ ~~~~ *Leadership*

"If you are warming to th~~e~~ side, then you should grab your own copy ~~~~ ~~~~ ~~E~~ven if you don't yearn for the highest ranks . . . this b~~~~ ~~~~ ~~u~~t smooth your everyday path through the organizational life."

—*Executive Bookshelf*

"Without losing academic rigor, the author brings a practical focus to the subject and . . . does not require the reader to be superhuman or to change personality beyond recognition. Professor Reardon successfully demystifies a subject that too often is used to create barriers to individual personal progress. It is likely that every reader will gain significant insight from the book, probably both at a personal level and in relation to the behavior of colleagues and organizations."

—Mary Walsh, PricewaterhouseCoopers

"We are all political animals. But politics exercised in a ham-handed manner can be unbelievably destructive to any organization, large or small. Here, Reardon shows us how we can apply politics, in the best sense of the word, toward personal, professional, and organizational success."

—José I. Lozano, publisher and CEO, *La Opinión*

"My first reaction was 'I wish I had read this when I was twenty-one!' But I quickly realized that it is just as useful to me today. This is an important book for anyone who hopes to maximize their personal power."

—Pete Hart, former CEO, MasterCard International

The Secret Handshake

The
Secret
Handshake

**MASTERING THE POLITICS
OF THE BUSINESS
INNER CIRCLE**

Kathleen Kelley Reardon, Ph.D.

New York London Toronto Sydney Auckland

The Secret Handshake was originally published in hardcover
by Currency in January 2001

A CURRENCY BOOK
PUBLISHED BY DOUBLEDAY
a division of Random House, Inc.
1540 Broadway, New York, New York 10036

CURRENCY and DOUBLEDAY are
trademarks of Doubleday, a division of Random House, Inc.

Please visit our website at www.currencybooks.com

Book design by Jennifer Ann Daddio

The Library of Congress has cataloged the hardcover edition
of this book as follows:

Reardon, Kathleen Kelley.
The secret handshake: mastering the politics of the business inner
circle / Kathleen Kelley Reardon.—1st ed.
p. cm.
Includes index.
1. Office politics. 2. Interpersonal relations. 3. Negotiation
in business. I. Title.
HF5386.5 .R4 2000
658.4'09—dc21
00-043216

ISBN 0-385-49528-5

PRINTED IN THE UNITED STATES OF AMERICA

First Currency Paperback Edition: February 2002

SPECIAL SALES
Currency Books are available at special discounts for bulk purchases
for sales promotions or premiums. Special editions, including
personalized covers, excerpts of existing books, and corporate
imprints, can be created in large quantities for special needs.
For more information, write to Special Markets, Currency Books,
280 Park Avenue, 11th floor, New York, NY 10017,
or e-mail specialmarkets@randomhouse.com

5 7 9 10 8 6

with love
to my children:

Devin—endearing comic, pianist, and
baseball base-stealing maverick

Ryan—always caring, imaginative, slugger
with enduring heart

Shannon—deeply affectionate, charming,
dancer extraordinaire

and Chris—my husband,
my best critic, my best friend

Acknowledgments

This book was a journey down an avenue not previously traveled at length. Politics is a critical aspect of business, yet it is an understudied one. So when Roger Scholl at Currency/Doubleday decided it was ground worth breaking, I couldn't have been more delighted. Roger's encouragement, energy, keen insight, and critical thinking were central to making this book possible. From the time we first talked, Roger exuded a confidence in this project and in me as a writer that made the process more enjoyable than it's supposed to be.

My agent, Peter Ginsberg, deserves my heartfelt gratitude for his constant interest in my research and its implications for practice. He was the first to see the potential in the topic of politics in the workplace. Over the years that I've worked with Peter, he has been both an agent and a mentor. He is not easily pleased nor happily diverted from the path he sees as having the most promise. He draws the best from his authors by hearing them out, suggesting, and encouraging. What more can an author ask of an agent? He is the best.

My children, Devin, Ryan, and Shannon, have watched Mom at the computer at all hours of the day and night. Yet we've spent many wonderful hours together for baseball, Cub Scouts, Brownies, dance, sports, and travel. Shannon now writes books of her own, telling friends that she is going to be a writer. Devin became my photocopying assistant and enjoyed it for nearly a hundred pages. His loving "How's it going, Mom?" often led to welcome writing breaks and discussions of the latest in a twelve-year-old's life. Ryan kept me company, playing Star Wars around, over, and under my feet, knowing almost instinctively when it was time to tone down the sound of fast-approaching enemy ships.

My husband, Chris, is a talented writer himself and has provided me with superb advice. He ignores reams of paper scattered here and there during intense writing periods and finds spare time away from his work to take a look at a chapter that I know is not quite there yet. My brother, Kevin, with whom I've coauthored articles on leadership, has talked with me at length about workplace politics. My sister-in-law, Susan, my nephew, Brian, and my niece, Meghan, have always been supportive of my writing endeavors; Brian even turns my books around on bookstore shelves so that the whole front cover is clearly visible. My mother-in-law, Connie, and father-in-law, Earl, provide not only support but also valuable insights. Jonathan, Kevin, Dennis, and Matt and my sisters-in-law Karen, Joan, Helen, and Tamre take a long-distance interest in my work and have shared political experiences of their own over the years. I am fortunate to have such a wonderful family.

At the University of Southern California Marshall School of Business, there are many people to thank. My years teaching in the

Executive MBA, International MBA (IBEAR), MBA, undergraduate, and executive education programs have helped shape this book.
My colleagues have inspired my thinking on the subject of politics.
Warren Bennis, leadership guru, also continues to have a significant
impact, as do the people who surround him and who made important contributions to Chapter 11 through speeches they gave at a
conference honoring Warren's career. Alan Rowe, professor emeritus
and expert in decision theory, influenced my views about leadership
and politics during our work together.

My gratitude extends to many communication scholars for their
superb research and writing, from my days as an undergraduate (and
later a faculty member) at the University of Connecticut with Martin
Hunt's encouragement, through M.A. and Ph.D. degrees from the
University of Massachusetts—Amherst, where Vernon Cronen, Jane
Blankenship, Jennings Bryant, Fern Johnson, and Barnett Pearce influenced my research, on through many International Communication
Association and National Communication Association presentations
and debates, where the ideas for this book were given form. Being a
communication scholar opens up so many fascinating avenues of
study. Politics is only one of them. After all, management itself is communication. There is nothing soft about this subject: it is the hard stuff
of business and of life in general.

My friends have also given me so much support. Ann and Larry
Marinovich provided me with wonderful stories and insights over
dinners and on our walks through Palos Verdes. Susan Daigh has
been there for me with ideas and connections to interviewees.
Thanks to Ellen Nichols, my dear friend of many years, who offered
both advice and support. Gail Fairhurst, across the miles at the
University of Cincinnati, has influenced my work by the genius of
her own. My good friend Marcy Pine made excellent suggestions

for interviews and took an abiding interest in the development of this book. Thanks as well to my friends Marianne Tegner, Nuala and Brian Egan, Tammy and Doug Scott, and Dierdre and John Lenahan. These kinds of friendships make writing enjoyable and determine its course in significant ways.

I want to thank my astute research assistant, Michael Sithole, whose research acumen was invaluable in ferreting out information from the most minuscule or unpromising of leads. I am grateful to those at Currency/Doubleday, especially Stephanie Land, with whom it has been a pleasure to work.

Special thanks to the senior executives, named, unnamed, and disguised, who opened their doors to me and spent precious time sharing experiences and political strategies. Their real-life political adventures made this topic live for me. Keen observers of human behavior like Betty Friedan, Mary Catherine Bateson, Edward Lawler, and Linda Fowler shared their perceptions of politics and, in so doing, influenced my approach and choice of subject matter.

Finally, I must mention my parents, from whom I learned much at the dining room table. They never shuffled me off to my room when they discussed the events of their workdays. That early exposure to politics and strategy formulation proved invaluable in later years when I encountered them along my own career path. This has made me a strong believer in allowing older children to hear political stories not only after they've occured but while they're unfolding. These life lessons provide a critical preparatory foundation for the later mastering of politics.

I have always been interested in relationships, especially at work. Without the sage advice and enduring support of the people mentioned here, I could not have written any book, let alone one that delves so deeply into the private strategies of hundreds of successful people, access to whom was often eased by a friend or a friend of a friend. Whether they assisted in making these connections, shared with me their own political successes and failures, or were just there to keep me on track, their generous help made *The Secret Handshake* possible. I am deeply grateful.

Contents

Introcduction

The term "secret handshake" refers to the acknowledgment one in-group insider gives another, conveying their shared distinction as members of the business inner circle. Those among us who acquire the coveted secret handshake become the "who" in "who you know." They're the comers, movers, and shakers, the ones who get the nod due to their exceptional technical competence, as well as an extraordinary ability to manage interpersonal relationships.

While there are a myriad of books on the technical skills needed to succeed in business, little attention has been paid to the equally important prerequisite of the secret handshake—political savvy. This is the hard stuff of business, the interpersonal skill that can never be totally or permanently mastered. The inner circles of business shift, as do the skills that get and keep people in them. Making it into one inner circle doesn't guarantee making it into another or into the most important one. The engineer who is promoted to senior vice president may never make executive vice president. He or she may be the best engineer in the company, but lack that extra something, the poise and professionalism, reliability and visibility that constitute a significant advantage on the road to the top. He or she may be unable to avoid or go around the interpersonal traps that ensnare so many otherwise competent people. In the final analysis too many questions may remain unanswered: Can he or she go the distance, handle the rough spots, inspire the troops, get the job done, and garner respect in the process?

This book is a journey toward that place where, for you, the answer to this question is an unequivocal yes. You'll emerge from this journey better apprised, better armed, more confident, and considerably more adept at mastering the interpersonal politics of work. Surely competence is critical to success; in fact, its very foundation. But technical competence is rarely sufficient. As Tom Peters says, "If you do not LOVE politics . . . then you will accomplish damn little." Politics, after all, is "the messy process of 'getting stuff done.'" If you can dispassionately decipher its workings, find "politics a hoot," then you've mastered an important step toward a powerful future.[1]

There are just too many smart, capable people out there. The hard truth is that the ones who get ahead are usually those who know how to make highly placed people feel good about having them around. The good news is that you can be one of them.

The Secret Handshake

1.

The Parameters of Organizational Power and Politics

———■———

There are two good reasons why the most coveted prize of business is called "the secret handshake." The first is that most people believe the political savvy necessary to break down barriers to the inner circles of organizations is inaccessible to all but a very few. That explains why there's a dearth of useful information devoted to the topic. Even organization experts consider politics an enigmatic puzzle. The second reason is that the path to the acquisition of this prize is purposely kept ambiguous by many of those who have successfully traversed it. They share sparingly the whereabouts and characteristics of the mazes, obstacles, and dangers that must be overcome in its pursuit. Some even deny that there is a path. After all, if just anyone could achieve the secret handshake, there would be no value in having attained it. It's an exclusive club, and certain conditions must be met for membership—certain hurdles overcome. Many of these hurdles have nothing to do with technical competence.

While the path to acquiring the secret handshake varies across organizations, both the existing research and the practical experiences of the many people I interviewed for this book indicate that *political savvy* is a prerequisite, more so even than job competence. This is especially true at higher levels of organizations where the signals are ever more ambiguous.

The prized executive offices are scarce, so competition is fierce. Yet at the loftier levels a high degree of professionalism is required. It's important for everyone to appear as though they are above pettiness and petulance. Consequently, political warfare at this level is subliminal and more often comprised of hidden minefields and stealth bombers than hand-to-hand combat. As the stakes get higher, the battle gets rougher, even if you can't see any weapons.

To the successful executive in a competitive organization, day-to-day life *is* politics. There is no doubt that a high level of field-based competence is needed to get ahead. But choose any two competent people, and the one who has political savvy, agility in the use of power, and the ability to influence others will go further.

Politics in the common vernacular refers to what other people do to get their way; as such it has negative connotations. Politics in organizations involves going outside the usual, formally sanctioned channels, something nearly every successful manager has done at one time or another. The real political moves are the ones not written down anywhere. Simply put, *politics is an illegitimate means of getting things done.*

So much of life is politics, especially at work. How should you approach a difficult situation? When should you take forceful action to stand up for yourself? How can you predict and prepare for others' reactions? Should you or shouldn't you fight a battle? If you do, how will you identify your allies and enemies? All these questions are part of daily life at work. As Caroline Nahas, managing director, Southern California, at Korn-Ferry International, sees it, there are two choices with regard to politics: "Either sit in the stands or get in the game and be a player." Yet Nahas doesn't see politics as necessarily—or even largely—negative: "To be politically astute, you need to read where the trend lines are, be ahead of the game, and focus on areas that you think will be important." There's nothing underhanded about this aspect of politics. In fact, it's constructive for the individual and the organization. Not all politics is so benign, however.

It didn't take Steve Harcourt, senior executive at a leading sports products company, long to learn this. As he describes it, he thought he'd been hired "to get all the money possible—to make a huge profit for the company." What he learned instead was that the CEO wanted increased profits but not at any cost. When Harcourt insulted one of the CEO's favored guys by suggesting that he do a few things differently, the response was not positive. Harcourt was edged out for a while. The CEO never said anything directly to him, but he got the message. He now believes, "If you ignore politics and make someone above you look bad, you're going to have a short career." So Harcourt's rule of thumb is to ask himself, "Can anything good come out of this?" That has gotten him the label of "political animal" at times, but as he sees it, politics is reality. You have to know when to speak up and when not to. Another Harcourt axiom: Don't tell the boss who doesn't want all the profits you could get for him that he isn't getting them. As Harcourt sees it, you have to know the primary goals and shape what you do to fit them.

Since political tactics aren't overtly sanctioned, they give rise to games that people play to build power bases, defeat rivals, and promote in-group members over those in the out-group. When such tactics work, over time they become embedded in the culture of the organization. At that point, few important things get accomplished in the absence of their application. Worse still, having gotten so used to playing games without having to think about how to do so, few if any of the people playing them are capable of articulating how they work. They can play them, but they can't explain how or why. They're like political robots irreversibly hardwired.

My primary aim in this book is to pull together the information gleaned from hundreds of interviews and probing discussions I've had with CEOs, senior managers, and high achievers in many fields during twenty years of business consulting, to shed light on how politics in organizations works. Moreover, I want to demonstrate how you can use political moves to gain admission to the inner circle of your organization—in short, to learn the secret handshake.

Politics and the Power Equation

While political strategies often operate in the service of wealth, they operate more often in the service of power—a resource for *getting things done* even in the face of resistance. The interesting thing about power is that it is often both a means to get ahead and the reward for getting there.

People who have valuable expertise, who control important resources or information, and those in positions of great authority not only can make things happen much more easily than those without power but also are in a position to increase their power and retain it. In order to win, the person engaging in politics need not always be the most powerful of those playing, but power does provide an advantage. It enables people to get things done even when others stand in opposition. Where one person has less formal power than others involved but accomplishes an objective nonetheless, it's likely that he or she used politics.

Power is at the heart of politics and may indeed *be* the heart of politics. Although power has a negative connotation for many people, it doesn't for those who've achieved the secret handshake. Without power they would not have made it. Without politics their sources of power would have been severely curtailed.

The Reciprocal Relationship Between Power and Politics

Even the most celebrated CEOs may never be far from losing power. A sharp drop in earnings, negative articles in *Fortune, Forbes,* or the *Wall Street Journal,* or the loss of key employees can bring them down a few pegs or even cost them their jobs. Unless they own the business outright, those executives whose power is supposedly unquestioned are wise not to believe it.

Bill Owens, president of a fast-growing video distribution company, discovered this when he hired an employee named Sam to take on some of the demands of the business. What Owens liked about his new right-hand man was his ability to handle things that clogged Owens's in-box. It appeared that Owens had found himself someone who could even run the show in his absence. When some of his people began to tell him that the perfect new hire had flaws, he assumed they were jealous. "I like to give my people room to fail, so I didn't pay much attention at first. Then I heard that Sam had been telling my people, 'Don't bother Bill with anything. Everything goes through me.' Some of my people warned me that I was giving him too much power. They claimed that he'd begun to say, 'I speak for Bill.' I thought it was a harmless exaggeration. After all, he was getting work off my desk."

It wasn't until a year had passed that Owens began to notice that what he called "the tone" of the company was changing for the worse. But he continued to tell himself that there was no way that such a competent, friendly, flattering person as Sam could be the problem. The increased workload seemed a more likely reason for employee unrest. "Sam stroked people, especially me. But I've since learned that he penalized anyone who tried to go directly to me. While he was flattering me, he was controlling them. He started telling my people, 'Bill's a great guy, but he forgets things.' Then 'Bill's a great guy, but he gets angry easily.' He told customers that he'd be doing something different soon, hoping to lure them away and start his own business. First he took the decision power, and then little by little he undermined my credibility with my employees and customers."

Eventually, Owens recognized Sam's intentions. During a six-hour wait for a tow truck when his car broke down on the way home from a ski trip, Owens realized that the warnings of his more loyal employees had been well founded. When he returned to work, he ousted Sam and spent the next few years undoing the damage.

Owens's experience demonstrates that even very experienced managers can overlook destructive politics. It also demonstrates that it's never too late to learn to recognize and respond to abuses of politics and power. Political savvy is a skill, not a trait. No one is precluded from acquiring it. Yes, there are some people to whom political acumen seems to come more easily than to others, just as some people learn languages or higher mathematics with greater ease than others do. Owens had to learn the hard way. But he's more alert now. The crucial fact here is that political savvy is an achievable skill for recognizing when politics is operating and for using those politics to your advantage. And it is a skill prerequisite to attaining the coveted secret handshake. So our next step is to define how to acquire it.

2.

Political Savvy

———————■———————

Being political at work garners two benefits that often outweigh the costs in terms of effort and difficulty. First, politics helps advance careers. To the extent that a person is achievement-oriented and works in an organization where politics flourishes, he or she will have to use politics to get ahead.

"I've had to become more politically sensitive as the company has gotten larger," a senior manager of a rags-to-riches-in-no-time-flat computer software company told me. "The people around here are getting so rich that they're even beginning to think they're competent. To get around them, I've had to be less direct, more strategic, and less up-front about my intentions."

The second benefit of knowing how politics works is self-defense. When politically inhibited people use politics, it's often more to protect themselves from others than to advance their own careers. Once the politically inhibited person becomes politically adept, regardless of the reason for doing so, he or she often finds that politics leads to rewards.

The Political Continuum

Whether politics is used to advance careers or for self-protection, the first step is discovering where you are on the political continuum, from the politically active on one end of the scale to the politically inhibited on the other end. Not only are the politically active comfortable with politics, they truly enjoy maneuvering around the rules to get things done. The politically inhibited, at the other end of the continuum, dislike political movers and shakers. They may play along to get along, as the saying goes, but they prefer not to do so.

The extent to which your position on the political continuum helps or hurts your career depends on the organizational culture in which you work. If an extremely politically active person works in an organization where politics is limited or discouraged, he or she is likely to be both unhappy and unwelcome. Intensely politically inhibited people who work in highly political organizations, divisions, or even offices can become equally unhappy and overstressed unless they find a protective mentor or a quiet niche in which to work.

Marcy Bergren Pine, a successful Los Angeles attorney, was politically inhibited early in her career. Nevertheless, Pine, who is now a partner in the prestigious law firm of Morrison and Foerster LLP, forged a path to success. Upon her graduation from Loyola she joined a leading law firm that, she freely admits, "needed a female attorney and I was it." This is where her conversion from being politically inhibited to politically active began. She came to appreciate the connections she could make in a high-profile law firm. In fact, as she soon learned, few things get done without connections.

As she reinvented aspects of herself in order to attain the rank of partner, Pine embarked on a campaign of impression management, not in order to be well liked, but in order to become respected and well connected. She changed her voice from "the social one I learned to use while being groomed for years to be a wife, to a lower-pitched, attorney-like voice. I stopped smiling so much and developed a little more of an edge, especially with aggressive businessmen and attorneys." Pine became an astute observer of the political landscape where she worked, and adjusted her actions to fit expectations. She set her sights on becoming partner and then proceeded to learn and do what it would take.

While sitting at a law firm dinner as a fifth-year associate with former secretaries of state and the interior William Rogers and William Clark, Pine realized that she had indeed arrived. "The most interesting thing," she said of the occasion, "is that I truly felt that I belonged there." The secret handshake had become hers.

For many people, politics is not just the ticket into the game but the means by which you come to decide which game is to be played. There is a time-honored view of success that says you're successful when the number of idiots under you is larger than the number over you. Alison May, COO at Esprit and former CFO of Patagonia, explains it this way: "I like to be the one ultimately making the call. I would much rather make a stupid decision and take the consequences than have to implement a stupid decision made by someone else. Therefore, I think I come across as someone confident, focused, and determined, because I am willing to accept the risks and negative consequences of being in a position of power."

Others, like Steve Delcarson, prefer to foster a team culture. Delcarson is a walking success story—and not just one. He has made a career of building companies with flat structures. He doesn't like working for other people, and, if he had his way, people wouldn't work *for* him either. "I'm against hierarchy in companies," Delcarson explains. "I much prefer team effort with everyone on the same playing field. You have to work within hierarchical contexts, but having people worry about who can go to whom about what when you're working on 'Internet time' isn't effective. I set the tone that politics doesn't exist in my companies, nothing behind the back, and no second agendas. If you're not comfortable, let's part ways."

But Delcarson isn't naive about politics. He admits to falling prey early on to the attraction of power. "You have to watch out that you're not becoming arrogant when you're successful, especially if it happens early on in your career." Delcarson is now a product of what he calls the "new school" of business thinking where leaders surround themselves with people more knowledgeable than themselves. He runs into politics but manages the work climate to minimize the effects. "You can keep a company relatively nonpolitical by setting examples. If someone comes in the back door to me, I'll ask if they've talked to their boss first. If they say yes and didn't get anywhere, then I need to talk with that supervisor." Delcarson believes in keeping in the communication loop but not in doing so at the expense of relationships.

Even among people like Delcarson who decline to get involved in politics, political adeptness becomes attractive because it allows them to be included in admired groups. Some people have a high need for affiliation. If the people with whom they want to be affiliated use political means to achieve their goals, then they themselves are likely to follow suit. It's a sort of "political lemming" mentality:

Everyone else is political, so why not me? One of the most powerful pulls on human behavior is the desire for inclusion. If you look around you and everyone is playing games, it's difficult to stay off the field.

Another benefit to acting politically is the thrill of victory. A considerable number of people get a lot of pleasure from using politics successfully. They derive satisfaction from knowing that they have accomplished something at which other, less savvy people have failed. Political thrill seekers may be either harmless or quite dangerous, depending on how far they'll go to have political fun at others' expense.

The most common reason for engaging in politics is to defend yourself from other people. When those around you are playing heavy-handed or underhanded games, survival may require you to do the same. The politically defensive find themselves improving their political skills out of a need for protection. As a result, in time, they often get good at it, and before they know it, they're political animals born out of necessity.

Sizing Up the Political Arena

An important part of adeptly moving up through an organization is developing the ability to identify the type of political arena you're in. You may need to escape an arena that is not suited to your advancement, perhaps even while remaining within the larger organization. If you feel that you don't have the option to go where the political environment suits you, you'll need to get particularly good at using the kinds of politics that flourish where you work. Your career survival will depend on it.

Organizations vary in the degree to which politics is used to accomplish goals. Most of my consulting work involves identifying the politics that is blocking communication and productivity. Then the task is to replace these dysfunctional political habits with more functional ones. The first step is to know what type of political climate is prevalent in the company or division having difficulties. There are four types. The first is the *minimally politicized* organization where the atmosphere is amicable. I don't often find myself consulting for such organizations because conflicts are rare and usually don't last long. There is a sense of camaraderie—an absence of in-groups and out-groups. One person's gain is not necessarily seen as taking place at the expense of someone else. Rules are occasionally bent and favors granted, but in general, people treat each other with regard and don't often resort to underhanded politics to achieve personal goals. Such organizations are excellent environments for people who are uncomfortable with politics. Unfortunately, these organizations are more the exception than the rule.

One minimally politicized organization is Patagonia, the outdoor sports clothing firm based in Ventura, California. When the surf is up, employees go to the beach. You might find a child sitting on Dad's lap while he designs a new backpack. In fact, with an excellent child-care center on-site, parents routinely visit their children during working hours with little concern that coworkers will be annoyed. There is a family feeling, a benevolent, live-and-let-live atmosphere. Patagonia isn't politics-free, but it is certainly one of the most desirable places to work in the United States.

Moderately politicized organizations operate primarily on generally understood, formally sanctioned rules. Unsanctioned means of achieving individual and group goals are not unusual, but when these tactics are used, it is done in such a manner that their existence can be denied if someone were to complain. In other words, those who run moderately politicized organizations prefer to convey the impression that everything is done by the rules. When I work with such organizations, a considerable amount of denial of politics goes on before the behind-the-scenes rules emerge to become constructively addressed.

Conflicts are not unusual in moderately politicized organizations, but they tend to be of short duration and not pervasive. Such a culture discourages overt conflict. When conflicts appear to be excessive, sanctioned rules or cultural mores are called upon to provide resolution. This type of environment works well for people who'd rather not engage in daily politics, but who are capable of managing or living with what might be called "pockets of political activity."

I recently consulted for a company with a pocket of political activity. It was a midsize organization where senior management wanted to be fair to employees and make all of them feel they were part of a cohesive, fast-paced team. Accomplishments were often handsomely rewarded. Handling of conflict in peaceful ways was admired. Despite such laudable goals and actions, however, there was a distinct culture of distrust in one pocket of the company. A senior manager was so favored by the CEO that anyone who offended him could be punished by humiliation (gradually, and seemingly within the rules) or even terminated. In an effort to avoid becoming the next target, many people fed negative information to the favored senior executive about others they knew he disliked. Conflicts were manifested not in overt attacks, but in gossip and undermining activities.

When the CEO brought me in to help improve communication,

he didn't realize that the primary source of his problems was sitting at a desk only one office away from his own and that he had given that person the power to create political unrest.

Moderately politicized organizations often suffer from a kind of schizophrenia—professing a desire for one thing but rewarding another. This mixed-message environment has become known as "asking for A while rewarding B."[1] Even when intentions are good and senior management really wants a culture where A thrives, political machinations make it difficult for leaders to effectively reward desirable behavior. They continue to preach a desire for A while rewarding another type of behavior—B. A classic example takes place in academia where many universities and colleges ask professors to become great teachers when the well-known but unwritten rule for success is to publish in professional journals.

I did some long-term consulting for an engineering and precision manufacturing firm that operated in this "do what I say," not "what will get you ahead," mode. On paper, the senior execs had open-door policies, but hardly anyone utilized the option. Why? Because, as one manager explained, "Here the rule to live by is, if you have an opinion keep it to yourself until asked." Several people had thought that the open-door policy actually meant that new ideas would be welcome by senior management, but it only took a few casualties for people to realize that "the tall tree catches the wind." Stick your neck out and it might not be there tomorrow.

I was in this company to help change the culture, to improve communication, reward people for making important suggestions, and encourage information sharing. It took a little bleeding on the carpet before we could move forward. A lot of people had bottled up a good deal of angst. The CEO I worked with allowed some bloodletting and even a few fingers pointed at him. That garnered him a lot of respect and facilitated the change efforts.

Smaller, fast-moving companies and the larger ones like Cisco Systems that try to stay agile tend to fall into the moderately political domain. They have a make-mistakes-and-move-on philosophy that keeps them from watching what everyone does. There's politics to be sure, but most of the time it's focused on how to get ideas to the fore rather than on how to play along to get along. Molly Tschang manages acquisition integration in the corporate development group at Cisco. She loves working there. The company is too big now to say that it isn't political, but she sees it as "an inspired, work-hard, kick-butt environment." In the twenty-three months after she joined the team, Cisco acquired a record thirty-five companies and the pace was ramping up steadily. "Cisco is a push-it-to-the-limits company," says Tschang. "We all take calculated risks and in doing so make mistakes—just not the same one twice. Cisco has an extraordinary culture where focus on the customer, results, teamwork, and trust matter most." It's this kind of focus that keeps companies of Cisco's size from becoming highly political.

In the third type of organizational political culture, the *highly politicized,* conflict is frequent and often pervasive. Formally sanctioned rules are only invoked when convenient, rather than being applied consistently across situations and people. In-groups and out-groups are clearly defined. Lots of topics are taboo, and you need to know what they are if you want to survive. Few people talk with the CEOs or their direct reports in these companies. Who you know is more important than *what* you know. Working in such organizations is highly stressful, especially for those who haven't figured out the games or who belong to one of the out-groups.

The leadership at one small but highly regarded organization I consulted at was fearful that one of its departments was about to implode. The department had always been a highly political place, but by the time I arrived, the situation had become serious. Cliques had formed. The young professionals were at odds with the more senior ones. Each group was regularly sending representatives to senior management to advance their agendas. People would slip into each other's offices to share the latest offense of the out-group and plan their interceptions and revenge. Work was still getting done, but the senior executive who asked me to help was right in his assessment that it was only a matter of time before clients would notice and complain. As I interviewed the members of the department, it became clear that while *initially* the person blamed for the conflicts was part of the problem, he was no longer the actual problem.

In point of fact, rarely is the person at whom fingers are pointed when I arrive at a company the single source of political unrest. Politics is relational. For every move that is made, countermoves occur. Thus even if only one or two people initiate conflict and political methods of interaction, in time others are pulled into the mix. One effective way to turn around this kind of situation is to help those involved recognize how each of them is contributing to the situation, and then work with them to break up old patterns and change how they relate to one another. Most organizations don't have the patience for this resolution process. It's easier to blame people and get rid of them. In highly politicized arenas, though, this quick-fix approach rarely alters the underlying pattern of dysfunctional politics.

Finally—and my condolences if you've ever worked in this political climate—there is the *pathologically politicized* organization. Such organizations, be they companies, agencies, or departments, are rarely as productive as they could be. Daily interactions are fractious. Conflict is both long-lasting and pervasive. Nearly every goal is achieved by going around the formal procedures and organization. People tend to distrust each other. Information massaging is the only form of communication. Out of necessity, people spend a lot of time watching their backs and covering their backsides. For this type of politicized organization, a quick demise is most merciful. As management expert Henry Mintzberg explains: "Much as the scavengers that swarm over a carcass are known to serve a positive function in nature, so too can the political conflicts that engulf a dying organization serve a positive function in society. Both help to speed up the recycling of necessary resources."[2]

I was once asked to help a group of stock exchange traders reduce their level of conflict with each other. All of them were young, bright, and capable, but they despised each other and competed unrelentingly. The most common form of interaction was the exchange of surface pleasantries accompanied by jabs and outright "sleazing." It got to the point where when a trader missed a meeting of an important task group, another one—who wasn't even a member of the group—attended the meeting in his place and used the opportunity to disparage his absent colleague. Ultimately, although a number of the traders reduced their tendency to resort to underhanded political tactics to advance themselves, the most incorrigible offenders had to be reassigned to other areas of the company. Their pathological political machinations had become ingrained. Leaving them in the same relationships would only have exacerbated the unhealthy conditions.

Such pathological arenas are often characterized by a carrot-and-stick approach to getting people to do their jobs. In the classic *Harvard Business Review* article "Asinine Attitudes Toward Motivation," Harry Levinson described this as the "jackass fallacy."[3] Subordinates are treated as if they need to be manipulated and controlled because they are seen as stubborn, stupid, and willful. This is in contrast to an organized system for rewarding achievement that advances the interests of the organization. The trouble with the "jackass" approach, Levinson pointed out, is that employees inevitably respond by trying to get as much of the carrot as they can, while avoiding the stick. If you find yourself constantly wielding sticks or dangling carrots in front of those reporting to you, then you may need to ask yourself whether it has simply become a bad habit that leads to little in the way of real, long-term achievement of important tasks. If you're the person who is spending a lot of time chasing the carrot or avoiding the stick, ask yourself whether you may be putting too much power in the hands of people who don't have your best interests in mind.

The four types of political arenas—minimally, moderately, highly, and pathologically political environments—can and usually do coexist within a single organization. It's possible to find a pathological department housed within a moderately politicized division, which is in turn embedded in a minimally or highly politicized organization. Moreover, political climates can change. Several of the people interviewed for this book said they'd love to know what to look for as warning signs of an impending negative political climate. Here are some of them:

Tell-Tale Signs of Cultural Pathology
in Organizations

1. Frequent flattering of those in power coupled with abu-
siveness toward people in less powerful positions is a sure
sign of creeping organizational pathology. Flattery may
not get you everywhere, but it is often used by those who
fear they cannot advance on their own merits.

2. Another sign of cultural degeneration is information massaging. When no one says anything that might rock the
boat, you can be sure that the organization is becoming (if
it isn't already) pathological. When people communicate
via hint instead of directly expressing their views, the roots
of pathology are present even if they haven't yet taken
over.

3. "Poisoning the well," which we'll discuss at greater length
later, is another political activity indicative of pathology in
organizations. The thing to look for is people frequently
fabricating negative information about others. They drop
defaming information into conversations and meetings in
the hope of ruining the target's career chances. Gossip and
verbal backstabbing are common here. There may be little overt conflict, but under the surface the organization is
seething with angst.

4. Some organizations are poisoned by the people in charge.
There's no need to poison the well. In such organizations
there's a cold indifference. No one is valued; in fact, every-

one is dispensable—and feels that way. The only way to survive is to become obsequious to those in charge and to get someone else before he or she gets you.

5. Whenever there is a good deal of "fake left, go right" strategy—leading others in the wrong direction in order to look good oneself—organizational pathology can be found. A sense of organizational teamwork is absent as individuals' careers are sacrificed to save those who are misleading them. Sometimes teams mislead teams, with the spoils going to the victor—the team that faked the best.

Once you have armed yourself with an understanding of how organizations vary in terms of political climate and some of the signs of increasing pathology, you are ready to look at who has a good chance of making it into the coveted inner circle in each type of environment. To determine this, we'll turn our attention to *individual* political style.

3.

Knowing Your Political Style—and When to Change It

———■———

Being able to identify and understand both your own political style and that of those around you lies at the heart of political success. So, too, does the ability to adapt your own style to that preferred by the people running the division and/or organization in which you work.

Ted Gambogi is sales vice-president for Maritz Marketing Research Inc. Earlier in his career, while working at another company, Gambogi learned that his boss had been replaced by the boss's archrival. This event provoked a crisis for Gambogi, who was immediately viewed by his new superior as a disciple of the previous boss. "Life became a continuous inquisition," Gambogi recalled. In addition, his personal style clashed with that of the new manager. Recognizing the seriousness of the situation, Gambogi fought the urge to vigorously defend his views and endeavored to alter his independent, take-charge style. "I undertook the practice of exhibiting empathy and proving my worth instead of fighting him day to day. I dedicated myself to achieving results that made him look good. I kept him in the loop and provided him with my constant support." The effort eventually succeeded, a dire situation was turned around, and Gambogi ultimately developed a good relationship with his new boss.

It may be impossible for a leopard to change its spots, but as Gambogi's experience shows, it's possible to stretch your style to accommodate the situation at hand. This adaptability is a crucial political skill. Mary Walshok, associate vice chancellor for public programs at the University of California, San Diego, and co-founder of UCSD *Connect,* which brings entrepreneurs and global resources together to strengthen the San Diego community, puts it this way: "There are no single leaders anymore. There's the deal maker, the glad hander, the hands-on person and so on. The same skills matter but in new ways. You need to know how to get things done, how to deliver." According to Walshok, few people achieve this goal on their own. We're all specialists. "Today's model should be a basketball team," Walshok says, apologizing a bit for the sports metaphor but assured of its application, "not a relay race." That means that only rarely does anyone need be an all-encompassing leader. But everyone needs to know what team role suits them best and also the types of environments in which they're likely to thrive. To do so, it's important for each of us to identify both our technical talents and political style preferences.

In order to control and direct your own political style, you first need to know to which style you are predisposed. Research in organizational politics has helped to identify four basic styles: Purist, Team Player, Street Fighter, and Maneuverer. Most of us are more inclined toward one style or the other, but you can learn to adapt your style to the situations in which you find yourself.

The Purist

The Purist believes in getting ahead through hard work. He or she declines to participate in politics, relying largely on the sanctioned rules to get things done. Purists are usually honest—indeed sometimes naively so. They firmly believe that getting ahead is a matter of simply doing your job well. Purists trust other people, so they prefer to work with others who do the same. For them, work is not about personal advancement at the expense of others, but about getting the job done well. In the right environment, they reason, personal advancement follows from such achievement. Behind-the-scenes grappling for power and prestige is not of interest to the true Purist.

I've met a few Purists at high levels of business, but not many. Politics is simply too pervasive in most organizations for career advancement based solely on competence. Many entrepreneurs are Purists. They leave large corporations to escape having to play games that they perceive to be irrelevant to their job. Chris Noblet, former PR director who is now an independent writer, is an example. "I just don't have the stomach for it. I learned from an expert how politics works. One of my bosses was a natural political animal. She knew all the moves. Butter wouldn't melt in her mouth. If accused of playing politics, she'd pull a 'Who me? Working together cooperatively for the interests of the company is what I do.' But she'd cut you if she needed to. You wouldn't want to turn your back."

Noblet survived by learning to identify the games and doing all he could to avoid participation. "I did my job very well and that mattered to them. But I also learned a few lessons from her. After a few years of watching her, I could play with the best of them. But I'll never be a natural. I went home at night tied up in knots. I never enjoyed the cut-and-thrust like she did."

The Team Player

The Team Player believes that you get ahead by working well with others and participating primarily in politics that advance the goals of the group. He or she declines to put personal career needs ahead of the group's needs. The Team Player, too, prefers to operate by sanctioned rules, although he or she isn't above trading favors or engaging in other relatively benign political games in the service of achieving team goals. Team Players are focused on getting the job done right and on creating conditions for team member advancement.

Kate Miller, senior executive at a leading temporary accountant placement firm, personifies the Team Player. I first got to know Miller when I consulted for her prior employer. At that time, Miller was not yet thirty years old and she was making $300,000 a year. Too busy to pursue an M.B.A. degree, she asked me to become her coach. Throughout our work, I was always impressed with her search for the best way to advance the company. What she lacked was a repertoire of ways to approach people and a tolerance for those who didn't say what they were thinking. "Dealing with a yes-person is a struggle for me," Miller told me. "I wonder why we're paying such people. Are they even thinking?"

This disdain for those who don't reveal what's best for the team is characteristic of the Team Player style. When the Team Player works with other Team Players, information sharing is common. But most work groups are a mix of style types. When I last talked with Miller, she was rethinking how her Team Player approach might be modified. "I'm going through a search-for-a-philosophy stage," she said. "When a company grows and you're growing too, the small-company atmosphere changes. People come in from larger companies who've played political games to survive. The landscape changes and you have to wonder if it isn't time for you to change too."

Don Shellgren in his thirty-six years with Transameric Life Companies managed to avoid the seedier side of politics by being a Team Player, ultimately becoming senior vice-president of corporate communications. He attributes much of his success to dedication and to having connected with people. "I've always been good at remembering people and what matters to them. If someone told me they were interested in something and I saw it at a swap meet, I'd pick it up and send it to them." And Shellgren admits he did some adjusting to each boss. "The first CEO was a golfer, so I took up golf. The next one was into tennis, so I got into that. Then the next CEO played racquetball, so I did too. But when a sky diver came along, I drew the line."

Despite these individual endeavors to please, Shellgren is in the Team Player category because his focus was always on the general good. The one thing Shellgren did that some might consider a bit political for a Team Player was that he always kept an eye out for where he'd thrive. "I learned early on that everyone you work for has exceptional strengths but also weaknesses. Many of my bosses were great one-on-one but not great writers. They wanted more public relations but weren't good at writing speeches. So I helped them. I always had a sense of where my boss needed help—where I could be the greatest asset by doing something differently than it had been done before."

Even the Team Player has to have a few political skills. Shellgren's best secret is that you should never be only one thing. "If you're not the best baseball player but you can play four positions," Shellgren advises, "the team will need you even if you're not a starter." By being valuable in a number of domains, Shellgren was able to stay out of the baser types of politics that might have been required if his skill level had been in question. "Especially today," he'll tell you, "the more arrows you have in the quiver, the more likely it is that they'll want you around."

The Street Fighter

The Street Fighter is an individualist who believes that the best way to get ahead is through the use of rough tactics. He or she is not at all inhibited in the use of politics. The Street Fighter relies more on subliminal politics than the Purist and the Team Player, but is just as likely to impose sanctioned rules when those rules serve personal goals. Street Fighters watch their backs, push hard to get personal goals achieved, and are slow to trust others.

Street Fighters thrive on what management consultant Brian Egan describes as the "cut-and-thrust" of business. They enjoy intrigue and derive personal gratification from working the system. When Egan described one such person to me, an accountant who "kept an ear to the doors," I asked him whether he considered this man to be devious. "Not at all," he said. "He was a lovely man." But the accountant believed in protecting himself and the many persons around him by keeping himself fully informed about what was going on and by managing some of it himself. Street Fighters don't allow themselves to remain ignorant of new developments. They don't enter an organizational dark alley unless they have investigated the terrain and are prepared to defend themselves. They're not out to "get" people nearly so much as they are determined not to be "gotten" themselves.

Fred Nicholas, chemist and senior researcher for a leading aerospace company, refers to himself as a Street Fighter. "I'm not saying I'm good at it, but I do it for survival," Nicholas says. "I don't sacrifice other people, but I believe firmly that in organizations Machiavelli rules. You survive by keeping on the offensive. You need to have a sense of what is going on in the company and where you can make an incremental gain."

Nicholas became a Street Fighter because he worked in organizations where it was typical. "One time a guy actually belly-bumped one of my guys into a wall during a discussion. This was typical. Lots of one-upmanship. People thrived on bringing up negative recent events about other executives. The president allowed this to happen. It became part of the culture, made worse by people who came and went, all operating just below the veneer. The company cut people without telling them. They'd come to work and find they'd been fired. It happened to me. But I'd been sick on the Friday they let a bunch of us go, so I showed up the following Monday. I got a severance check. I was the lucky one. Three days later the place went bankrupt and the others got nothing."

Street Fighters usually emerge from such backgrounds. They've been burned often enough to know that life can be tough, so they play tough. Nicholas sees it this way: "If you haven't been through these things, it probably scares the hell out of you. If you've been through it, life is good because you're always ready."

Teri Dahlbeck, president of Got Marketing, an emerging

Internet business, is another Street Fighter. Dahlbeck believes, "The most effective people are Street Fighters. If you ask people what I'm like, they say 'a go-getter, someone who'd run over her own grandmother.'" In reality, Dahlbeck has Team Player leanings too. She enjoys bringing her team along, having their product succeed, and she denies that she'd run over her grandmother or anyone else. It's an image she's gotten from fighting hard. Like Nicholas, Dahlbeck had a rough past. She was at Apple Computer when it was "the worst time to be there. You couldn't go a day without feeling you were in a sick environment. It was eat or be eaten. CEO turnover was constant, as it was for the people around them. Instead of focusing on productivity, everyone focused on how to still have a job, and how to strategically align. I made sure I knew what the higher-ups wanted and made sure I could deliver." Her only regret is not leaving that environment sooner. "I was so involved in the street fighting I lost sight of the product which I'd been passionate about."

The Maneuverer

The Maneuverer is an individualist, one who believes in getting ahead by playing political games in a skillful, unobtrusive manner. He or she is not at all inhibited about using politics to advance personal objectives and favored team objectives, but prefers to do so in deniable ways. The Maneuverer looks for ulterior motives in others, has little regard for sanctioned rules, relies largely on subliminal politics, and is more likely to be a subtle operator than the Street Fighter. Maneuverers might be called "smooth operators." They're less committed to hard work than Purists, and only operate as Team

Players when it suits their agendas. If people get in the way of a Maneuverer, it is at their own peril.

Many people I interviewed are Maneuverers, but few want to be identified as such. One of them, whom I'll call Frank, started his career at IBM and moved to a small, fast-paced entrepreneurial venture. In his early years, he learned that impressions could be manipulated to his advantage. "I set fires and put them out. Then I was a hero. I'd create a problem and solve it. I've gotten promoted every one and a half years this way. The way I see it, if you don't leverage yourself, you're lost."

Frank and people like him are not so much out to harm other people as to advance their own careers. Are there friendly, caring Maneuverers? Yes, there are some. And there is a lot of the Maneuverer in a lot of Street Fighters and Team Players. The latter aren't comfortable with maneuvering others, but they can stretch to meet the demands of a situation. Even Purists can stretch now and then if they teach themselves to do so. That's part of what this book is about—teaching yourself to stretch beyond your preferred style by using strategies you'll learn in future chapters. But first, it's important to know whether your style preferences fit within the culture of your organization.

Fitting Your Style to the Organization

You can't achieve the secret handshake in an organization that is completely antagonistic to your style. Therefore, it's crucial to know if you're in the right kind of place to get ahead. Your individual political style will interact in predictable ways with the political culture where you work, affecting your chances of success.

The table below is more of a general guide than an absolute prescription.[1] If you're a Team Player, for example, you might be able to tough it out in a pathological organization where, on the surface at least, there are rewards for teamwork. The likelihood of your achieving the secret handshake in that place, however, is very low. In fact, regardless of your style, investing your effort in an organization for which you're unsuited is not a pleasant or productive way to spend a chunk of your life.

Fit of Style to Organization Type

STYLE	POLITICAL ENVIRONMENT			
	Minimal	**Moderate**	**High**	**Pathological**
Purist	Best fit	Possible	Unlikely	Highly unlikely
Team Player	Likely	Best fit	Unlikely	Highly unlikely
Street Fighter	Highly unlikely	Likely	Best fit	Possible
Maneuverer	Highly unlikely	Possible	Best fit	Likely

Purists, for example, are best suited to minimally political arenas, where they are likely to thrive. If a Purist finds herself in a moderately politicized environment, she may be able to survive by finding a niche where she can work while remaining out of the line of fire. She's not, however, very likely to be promoted to senior levels in such an organization.

Team Players function best in minimally to moderately politicized organizations. They may encounter significant difficulty in highly politicized areas where most people are out for themselves. In a pathologically politicized environment—the worst possible case—

the Team Player is in big trouble and should concentrate on finding a survival niche while looking for a new job.

Street Fighters are unlikely to be welcome in minimally politicized arenas, where people prefer to get along and tend to avoid overt conflict. They can work well in moderately political arenas, but they will need to tone down their inclination toward conflict. The best place for Street Fighters is the highly politicized environment, where they will thrive precisely because they have few or no compunctions about using politics to get things done and advance their careers. If they are also capable of expert maneuvering, they could well survive in pathologically politicized arenas too.

Maneuverers often function effectively in moderately politicized environments and best in the highly politicized. On the other hand, they may be surprised to find themselves unpopular or even despised in minimally or even some moderately politicized arenas. In such circumstances, they must essentially operate under cover much of the time. Their manipulative tendencies make it possible for them to succeed in pathological environments, especially if they are sufficiently expert in deception.

Why Do Organizations Tolerate and Promote Politics?

If organizations did a better job of suppressing or discouraging politics, wouldn't politics disappear? Wouldn't things be better? People who dislike playing politics often hope for this. "If senior management would only take responsibility for minimizing politics," they say, "the rest of us hard workers could just sit down and get our jobs done."

Some organizations do indeed attempt to modify the influence of politics in their operations. IBM's chief executive officer, Lou Gerstner, introduced the concept of "straight talk." Employees of Big Blue are expected to replace the obfuscating techniques of hint and innuendo with more direct forms of communication. To some extent, this has been effective. "At its best," one IBM executive told me, "even the most junior IBM employee can preface a comment by saying, 'In the interest of straight talk,' and everyone—up to the most senior person present—will listen."

At another corporate behemoth, General Electric, CEO Jack Welch has taken forceful steps to halt a natural tendency of employees to hoard ideas. Whereas in most companies individual advancement is often expedited by revealing great ideas at the propitious moment—for example, at meetings when senior people are present and more likely to notice you—Welch doesn't tolerate such methods. According to Steve Kerr, director of GE's Leadership Development Training, if you tell Jack Welch an idea, the first thing he'll ask is how many other people have you shared it with. If you admit to telling no one else, you might as well not have mentioned that great idea at all. After all, Welch's reasoning goes, if an idea is good enough to bring up to the CEO, it's good enough to have been surfaced, shared, and tested in a variety of contexts.

Such efforts to diminish dysfunctional politics and their ill effects can often be quite effective. However, they can never entirely rid an organization of political games. For every political game that is diminished or stamped out, another takes its place—it's just human nature. Even when political games are no longer visible on the organizational landscape, they may well be operating just beneath the surface. The best that organization leaders can do is to monitor and attempt to manage the level and types of politics. And no matter what positive steps your organization takes to manage its political culture, you will still need to keep abreast of what is actually going on politically and, if you want to stick around, adapt your style to fit. The next several chapters describe how.

4.

Profiling the True Political Player

———— ■ ————

There is a set of perspectives possessed by those who have made it into the inner circles of their organizations; they share ways of thinking that position them to be noticed and appreciated. This chapter examines this set of perspectives and, in so doing, provides a profile of the true political player.

The Need to Lead

General Norman Schwarzkopf, leader of Operation Desert Storm, which brilliantly swept the invading Iraqi army out of Kuwait in 1992, began his career with the need to lead. "I did not come into the army to be a lieutenant, or a captain, or a major," he has said. "I always thought I was going to be a general. At least I always intended to be a general. So I always aimed high. My sights were always set very high. I always dreamed high."

Schwarzkopf considers leadership something that must be done passionately, something one must feel deeply about. He once walked through a minefield to reach a wounded soldier who was screaming and writhing on the ground. Concerned that the soldier might set off more mines or cut another artery in his leg and die, Schwarzkopf explained, "I had to go over there and settle him down. There was nobody else to do it, so I had to walk through the minefield."[1] He doesn't see his act as heroism so much as simply the kind of leadership he had to assume at the time. This is how a true player thinks: Get out there and do what others won't or can't do.

It's rare for someone to go far in business without a strong desire to get his or her ideas across, to influence, motivate, and direct others. Those who aspire to lead a team, even in quieter ways, are far more likely to reach the inner circle than those content to follow. What about those obsequious followers who have little talent, yet obtain high-level positions? With few exceptions, they tend to fail over time, and their lives are often ones of quiet desperation, because what they usually have going for them is the favor of a single highly placed, vulnerable person. True "players" don't make it to the top by hanging onto other people's coattails, at least not for long. They take calculated risks. They need to *lead,* and they realize that one can't do that by cowering in the rear of the crowd.

When to Lead and How

There's a tendency to equate leadership with command, even in team-based organizations. Yet leadership comes in many forms. And political players carefully assess which form works for each situation in which they find themselves.

Sometimes the best leader is one who doesn't appear to be leading at all. Yogi Berra and George Steinbrenner hadn't spoken to each other in fourteen years after a personal row between the New York Yankee great and the team's controversial owner. Most people were content to let sleeping dogs lie, but not sports radio host Suzyn Waldman. Berra, who had played for ten World Series championship teams with the Yankees, had vowed to never again set foot in Yankee Stadium after Steinbrenner fired him as the Yankee manager just sixteen games into the 1985 season.

Waldman arranged for the two antagonists to meet at Yogi Berra's baseball museum on the campus of Montclair State University in New Jersey. Waldman so skillfully arranged and timed the meeting, remaining watchfully in the background as the men spoke for the first time in years, that Steinbrenner took the opportunity to apologize to Berra, who accepted graciously. Immediately following the reconciliation, Berra and Steinbrenner appeared together on Waldman's show, which was broadcast live from the museum. It was a big coup for Waldman, whom many sports fans, players, and rivals had resented for her unrelenting determination to break the unwritten rule that sportscasters must be men.[2]

As Waldman's story indicates, it's important to recognize that leadership doesn't always take the form of visible command, nor should it. True political players know this. They know there are times when leadership requires a logical approach, a visionary approach, or even a supportive one.

How, then, do political players assess which style is likely to work best in a given situation? Certainly they listen well; but that's not enough. A lot of people listen well, but they don't know how to assess the styles of those around them and adjust their styles to create a good fit. This skill sets political players apart. They've trained themselves to hear not only *what* people say but *how* they're saying it. From this they determine a person's style. If you aren't already proficient at identifying styles, there is a way to hone your skill—a method for recognizing style types first by an "inventory" and then by conversations.

Below, you will find the Leadership Style Inventory (LSI), which was developed at the Marshall School of Business by myself and colleagues Alan Rowe and Warren Bennis.[3] This inventory has been administered to hundreds of executives and managers at workshops and seminars we've conducted in recent years. The match of inventory findings with self-reports of their styles by those who used the LSI is quite high—above 95 percent. Complete and score the inventory, and you'll learn which types of leadership are the most comfortable for you at this time in your career. We've found it to be a powerful tool for managers in terms of seeing how they're predisposed to lead and whether these predispositions match those of the people who have reached the inner circle in their organizations.

LEADERSHIP STYLE

To score the instrument, use the number 8 for the response that is MOST like you, a 4 for the one that is MODERATELY like you, a 2 for the one that is a LITTLE like you and a 1 for the response that is LEAST like you. DO NOT REPEAT any number when answering a given question. You MUST use all of the four numbers when responding to a question. THERE ARE NO RIGHT OR WRONG ANSWERS so respond with what comes first to your mind.

1. I see my role as:	establishing objectives	specifying new directions	making goals exciting	listening to people	
2. I prefer an organization:	that has a strong work ethic 1	that adapts easily to change 2	that values people with new ideas 4	that provides support 8	
3. I expect my associates to:	be loyal 1	be reliable 4	recognize my contribution 2	be team players 8	
4. To gain commitment, I	provide incentives 8	rely on logical arguments 2	create a feeling of trust 4	enable performance 1	
5. I expect people to:	show initiative 2	persevere in their work 4	feel a sense of job ownership 8	participate with others 1	
6. Power is needed to:	maintain control 1	achieve objectives 8	facilitate restructuring 4	assure responsibility 2	
7. I think that people should:	be self-confident 8	be logical 2	have daring ideas 1	work well with colleagues 4	
8. To improve performance, I	insist on meeting goals 2	offer challenging assignments 4	rely on the team approach 1	assure fair rewards 8	
9. I look for:	personal status 8	job fulfillment 4	dignity and respect 2	acceptance 1	
10. Change requires:	concrete actions 2	the right timing 4	understanding people's needs 8	a feeling of security 1	
11. Successful people are:	hard-driving 4	competent 8	creative 2	effective communicators 1	
12. I value:	accomplishment 4	responsibility 2	radical change 1	personal growth 8	
13. Others see me as:	committed to my work 4	being a good problem solver 1	having broad vision 2	being a team player 8	
14. I try to be:	concise 2	thorough 1	open minded 4	sensitive 8	
15. Performance depends on:	following orders 4	consistent plans 8	creating opportunities 2	a feeling of trust 1	

16. Organizations should:	have well-defined plans ⁴	insist on quality output ²	encourage collaboration⁰	build shared values ¹
17. When there is a problem I:	take charge ¹	explore my options ²	network with my colleagues⁸	consult with others ⁴
18. I admire people who:	are efficient ⁸	are flexible ²	are imaginative ¹	are dependable⁴
19. I constantly try to:	work hard ⁸	plan ahead ²	find new approaches ¹	learn from others ⁴
20. I feel it is important to:	achieve results ⁸	be accurate ²	expect cooperation ¹	appreciate others ⁴

© Alan J. Rowe, Kathleen K. Reardon and Warren Bennis, rev. 7/25/1995 (This form may not be reproduced without written permission)

82   65   71   82

After you've completed the inventory, add each of the four columns, and place the totals at the bottom of the columns. Your four scores should add up to 300. The score at the bottom of the first column on the far left is your *Commanding style* score. The second column is your *Logical style* score, the third is your *Inspirational style* score, and the fourth is your *Supportive style* score. As you can see from the table below, each of these styles differs in terms of how people focus, persuade, introduce change, and learn.

Styles of Leadership

STYLE	FOCUSES ON	PERSUADES BY	INTRODUCES CHANGE	LEARNS BASED ON
Commanding	Results	Directing	Rapidly	Rules and policies
Logical	New direction	Explaining and reasoning	Incrementally	Questioning
Inspirational	New opportunities	Creating excitement	Radically	Experimentation
Supportive	Facilitating work	Encouraging involvement	By consulting with others	Gaining acceptance

© 1993, 1995 by A. J. Rowe, K. K. Reardon, and W. Bennis.

Commanding types want to get things done. They are inclined to direct people to action rather than persuade them with extensive reasoning. They spend little time observing, except for those who also score relatively high on Logical. If you scored 86 or more on Commanding, you are above the mean.

By contrast, *Logicals* assess situations carefully before moving to action. They persuade by providing reasons and walking people through what they consider to be compelling logic. They aren't quick to make changes because they want to be sure they've taken into consideration all relevant data. If you scored above 80 on this style dimension, you are above the mean.

Inspirational leaders are attracted to radical change. They like to think beyond the obvious to come up with creative ideas and rarely have patience with regard to implementing those ideas. To persuade others, they empower and excite them. The mean Inspirational score is 81.

Supportive leaders are inclined to help people follow the path others agree is the best one. They persuade others by making it easier for them to believe in and follow that path. They are slow to make changes because they want to be sure that issue-relevant people are pleased with any proposed moves. The mean score for this style is 65.

Each of us has a primary style predisposition, as well as backup styles. If, for example, you scored above 86 on Commanding and above 65 on Supportive, then you are likely inclined to be firm, direct, and quick to change, but you also try to help people feel good about and succeed at following your lead. Supportive is a backup style for you. If you scored above 80 on Logical and high on Commanding as well, then you are someone who reasons through decisions, looking at the pros and cons, but once you've done so, you take action.

Logicals with a Supportive backup style not only think through potential actions carefully but do so in terms of who will be pleased and who displeased. If you scored high on both of these, you are surely not the impulsive type. If you're Logical with a backup Inspirational style, you are thoughtful about change but also attracted to creative ideas. If an idea is attractive enough, you may even put aside your logical focus and take a chance. A Commanding backup style means, as mentioned previously, that you think carefully before taking important actions, but once you've gotten the data you need, you move quickly to implement what seems to you the most practical action.

Those whose highest score is Inspirational, with a backup style that is Commanding, particularly fit the profile of an entrepreneur. In our research we've found that successful entrepreneurs tend to have creative ideas (Inspirational) and the determination to carry them out. Inspirationals with strong Logical backup scores are creative but are less inclined than the Inspirational/Commanding type to move quickly, even if an idea is very appealing. And the Inspirational with a strong Supportive score creates excitement for people and makes change rapidly, but attempts to make sure others are equally enamored with the change.

Strong Supportives (above 65) with a strong Logical score would be the type to walk someone through their reasoning and to assist him or her in following their lead. Supportives don't rush to implement change because they want the buy-in of others. Strong Supportives with Commanding as a backup are rare. But we've found them here and there. They want people to be pleased with their decisions. Once they're sure of their support, they move quickly to implement plans. Supportives with a backup

Inspirational style seek the backing of others for their novel ideas and do so in a way that generates enthusiasm.

Those who need to lead employ their predispositions in ways that move them ahead. They look around and determine whether their styles, primary and backup, are hindering or helping this effort, and, when necessary, they stretch their styles to make their leadership efforts more effective.

"I recall having four new managers in a one-year period and having to posture until I better understood their individual managerial approach," John Richards, marketing director for a leading office products company, told me. "I normally am very direct internally. I recently discussed my career with my outgoing manager, and her comment was that she was surprised that I'd changed tactics in dealing with people who traditionally blocked my initiatives. I'd chosen a less direct approach than my usual frontal-assault method. What amazed me is that she didn't recognize that I had adapted to her style as a direct result of observing her and seeking her input."

Your leadership style is not etched in stone. It can be changed and stretched. For example, a Commanding person with a relatively high Logical score can easily play the role of the Logical leader if the situation calls for it. Commanding leaders can also be Supportive if they score relatively high on the latter style. While conducting a training session at Toyota, I spoke with a participant who had high Commanding and Supportive scores. She described herself as capable of being direct, assertive, and results-oriented, but she was also interested in achieving consensus when time pressures allowed.

Sharon Allen, managing partner for the Southern California/ Nevada practice of Deloitte & Touche, is a Logical. But that isn't her only style. "When I choose to be in charge, I'm in charge," she told me. "I am persistent and forceful when needed. At those times, people are very clear of my leadership." Allen sees her ability to stretch to a Commanding style as a real asset. "It works very well because I'm not always like this. So people sit up and take notice." She doesn't abandon her Logical side, though. "I'm never willing to accept something that doesn't make sense." In fact, it's when an action doesn't make sense that Allen tends to become Commanding to assure that the wrong path isn't taken.

How to Stretch Your Style

It's one thing to know that you *should* stretch your style to match those of the people in position to influence your career, and another to do it *well.*

Madeline Larson, senior executive at one of the largest U.S. banks, and Frances Larson, vice-president of public relations for a telecommunications giant, became successful by assessing how well their styles meshed with leaders in their organizations. "I used to not think about politics in the workplace," Madeline told me when the three of us met for an interview. "I came to realize that power and the ability to be successful politically involved filling a role needed at the particular point in time. I watched a woman self-destruct by being unpredictable and resisting change rather than fitting in. She asked thought-provoking questions in a way that made her appear to not be a team player. She used to say, 'Instead of embracing change, we should embrace progress.' They didn't see that as helpful." This woman clearly had a Logical leadership style, while the company valued Supportive team players.

Frances also had to make some leadership style alterations. She toned down her Commanding approach to managing others. "I've learned how to soften how I question. I might say, 'How about this as a solution?' I'm a person you shouldn't mess with, but I've also learned to be human and casual with people. I make a point to be attuned to how people are perceiving me and how they're being perceived. So I won't dress down a subordinate."

Madeline added, "I'm not a Janet Reno. I'm small and soft-spoken. I can be hard and firm, though. As a result, I was jarring people. My bosses counseled me but I resented it. So I got some coaching. It made me aware that I needed to be supportive when voicing criticism. I learned to say things like, 'I really agree with what Bill just said. But what if this were to happen?' I started doing well with my bosses but not so well with peers. So I learned to compliment them for what I wanted them to do [more Supportive]. Exclaiming 'Good question. What a great question!' or 'You're right and that works for the entire organization because . . .' proved useful. It felt a little manipulative at first, but it worked very well and soon became second nature."

True players are people who've adapted their leadership styles to fit the needs of their divisions or organizations. This requires the kind of skillful style tweaking that Madeline and Frances did, achieving the kind of balance that worked for them, allowing them to fit within the cultures of their organizations.

Here are examples of how this tweaking process works. The same idea can be conveyed in different ways, according to different leadership styles:

Example 1: Assume that at a meeting you were interrupted for the third time by a coworker. You could say:

Commanding: "Don't interrupt me again."

Logical: "Your interruptions are likely due to your enthusiasm, but there are some important points that need to be made here, so I'd like to finish."

Inspirational: "For the benefit of the whole team and to assure we find the best solution, we should be sure to give everyone a chance to speak."

Supportive: "Excuse me. I believe it will be helpful if I elaborate somewhat before we move on."

Example 2: You disagree with your boss. There's a pause in the discussion. You could say:

Commanding: "We're pressed for time here, so I'll just tell you why I think we're going down the wrong path."

Logical: "There's more than one way to look at this. From vantage point A it seems logical, but let's take a moment to look at vantage point B."

Inspirational: "I see your point. But there's an option we haven't explored that is very exciting."

Supportive: "I'd like to make what I believe is a constructive suggestion that builds on some things said earlier by you, Bill, and by Sue and Tim as well."

Notice that the Commanding options are brief and to the point. The Logical ones focus on explanations, Inspirational on team goals or an exciting possibility, and Supportive on making people feel comfortable. These examples show how stretching to each of the styles sounds and also demonstrate how you can identify style through conversation. After all, you can't hand people the LSI every time you want to discern their styles. By listening closely to how people talk, you can identify their style preferences.

Those who regularly make brief comments of instruction and focus on results are likely to have Commanding as their primary style. If they are prone to explain things, provide data, or persuade by reasoning, their preferred style is Logical. If they like to generate enthusiasm and use this to encourage people to follow them, they're Inspirational. And finally, if they tend to focus on making sure people are content with what they're proposing, they're likely Supportive. To the extent that your style meshes with that of people in a position to determine your future, you'll likely have a brighter one than people whose styles are a poor fit with those of their bosses.

Unless you have known people for a while, it's difficult to determine just how strong a particular style preference is for them, but if you are able to identify their preference by listening to them, you have the advantage of knowing which styles likely will and won't work with them. This is a powerful advantage.

Extreme Focus

Sitting at a beachside restaurant in Santa Monica with a visiting New York mover and shaker, I was surprised to find myself in a discussion of why my companion couldn't say no when people asked him for help. After all, he was a consultant to presidents and industry moguls seeking business-related advice.

"You know what they say," I said, sympathizing with his tendency to overload himself. "If you want something done, ask a busy person."

My dinner companion nodded, but then he looked me in the eyes and replied, "The way *I* see it, if you want something done, ask a *relentless* person."

He was right. True players tenaciously refuse to lose sight of their goals, even in the face of discouragement and rejection. One such person is Peter Samuelson, a highly successful movie producer who cofounded, with his cousin the actress Emma Samms, the Starlight Foundation, which provides wishes and services to seriously ill children. He also founded the Starbright Foundation, which provides mass media entertainment and education to children in hospitals, and more recently, First Star, which works in Washington, D.C., to draw attention to the legal needs and rights of children.

Whether he's convincing a prospective donor to help his foundations or pitching a movie idea, Samuelson says he can only sell that in which he truly believes. "If in your mind's eye you can't see how it will be, you'll never sell it—in charities or movies," he says. "I've never sold an iffy movie—only the ones I've truly believed in myself. But it hasn't ever been easy. Virtually everyone who says yes to me had earlier said no."

It was Samuelson's dogged determination that made the fledgling Starbright Foundation a reality. He asked for a meeting with Steven Spielberg, arguably the most powerful person in Hollywood today, and he got one. The meeting was scheduled to last only fifteen minutes. Once they were seated and talking in Spielberg's office, Samuelson began to earnestly and, yes, relentlessly describe how Starbright's efforts could change the lives of children who are facing the difficulties and fears of illness. In the end, Samuelson talked with Spielberg for several hours, and by the time he had finished describing the Starbright project and how it would help improve the lives of critically, chronically, and terminally ill children, the much-in-demand Spielberg was hooked. He not only agreed to become chairman of the Starbright board, but also made a sizable donation and later helped Samuelson connect with none other than General Norman Schwarzkopf, who agreed to become chairman of the Starbright Capital Campaign.

When he wants to get something done, Samuelson works at it until it happens. He is unrelentingly focused. As one of two professors asked by Samuelson to study Starbright's feasibility, I met frequently with him and his handpicked committee of L.A.-based entertainment and business executives. At every meeting, committee members came up with what they thought were compelling reasons why Starbright couldn't work. Samuelson was undaunted by this. He had selected them for the committee because he knew they wouldn't be yes-men. There were times when someone without Samuelson's fierce focus and determination would have thrown in the towel. But once our research indicated Starbright could indeed succeed, I knew that Peter Samuelson would make it happen: His energy and enthusiasm were contagious. Today, hundreds of thousands of families get information about their children's illnesses, support in their attempts to cope with disease, and special computerized entertainment that helps make the children's lives easier. The kind of focus Peter Samuelson exhibited is exactly what it takes to become a player in any field.

Ann Lewis used her ability to focus to reach the position of counselor to President Bill Clinton and then senior advisor to Hillary Rodham Clinton's Senate campaign. An untiring advocate for women's rights, she works long and hard to influence systems that stand in the way of equality. Lewis became a leader, she told me, because "I wanted to change the world, and I was determined to make a difference on behalf of the issues I believe in. People who get chosen for things make the rules, so I wanted to be one of them."

Working at Boston City Hall in the 1970s, Lewis discovered and became a staunch supporter of the women's movement. Since there wasn't a lot of money to help get messages out, it was there that she learned how to focus on her objectives, no matter what the obstacle. She found the people she needed to help advance the cause she believed in and didn't wait for them to invite her for a visit. "When you really want something," Lewis told me, "you don't wait to be invited."

When faced with critics, who are rife in Washington, Lewis stays focused. She doesn't tear herself apart with self-doubt or give up at the first sign of criticism. "I never second-guess myself . . . I wasn't raised that way. I don't dwell on things like that. If I make a mistake, I learn from it and move on." That kind of focus is fundamental in achieving the secret handshake.

Think Like a Chess Player

The second key aspect of the political player is advance thinking. No one becomes a chess champion without learning to envision the game several moves ahead, and no one enters the inner circles of business without that same almost prophetic ability. Politically adept people know how to learn the "lay of the land" so they can set about creating the conditions that will make their endeavors more likely to succeed.

Imagine you've just taken a new position. You walk into your first meeting and learn that of the five other people present, two are senior to you, two are at your level, and one is junior to you. They begin to discuss a problem with which they've been struggling for several months. It just so happens that in your most recent job you faced a similar problem. It was a thorny issue, so you're not totally surprised that the group hasn't yet arrived at the solution you already have in mind. You decide to propose your solution then and there. But as you finish telling them your ideas, you find, much to your surprise, they don't like them. Edward, one of the senior people, frowns. The junior person, Patrick, had written your ideas on his notepad, but then crossed them out after seeing the look on Edward's face. Michael, the other senior person, abruptly tells you, "We tried something like that once before and it didn't work." One of your peers, Susan, rolls her eyes, and the other, Paul, who was hired not long before you, doesn't say anything.

Should you try to re-cover ground? Should you explain your ideas more fully and then press for their adoption? After all, you've impressed other groups, as tough as this one, with your intelligence and powers of persuasion. Here, though, the fact is that you aren't being measured on your brilliance alone just yet. These people don't know you. They don't know where to place you on a number of evaluative dimensions. Consider the kinds of questions that could be running through their minds:

- Is this person really smart?
- Will s/he make me look bad?
- Is s/he a team player?
- Do people important to my career respect her/him?

- Does s/he think s/he can just waltz in here and start calling the shots?

None of these questions has much to do with whether or not the
ideas you offered are sound.

Take Susan, for example. She may be defensive as a rule. She
may consider herself the rising star. You could usurp her position.
She's concerned about feeling safe, not about how smart you are.
Then there's Patrick, who wrote your ideas down only to cross them
out when Edward, who may have considered your confidence a bit
premature, expressed displeasure. Perhaps Patrick is afraid of
Edward. To him you're already a liability. Michael rejected your suggestions out of hand because they've supposedly been attempted
before. You may discover later on that Michael is the idea gatekeeper
of the group. If you don't run an idea by him *before* a meeting, it
isn't going to survive. By speaking up too early, you gave him the
impression that you're a loose cannon rather than a team player and
that you're too smart for your own good.

Thinking like a chess player means finding out these kinds of
things before you offer your opinions. Spend a little valuable time
observing and you'll learn to go to Michael with your idea before
the meeting, to invite Susan in on promoting it so she looks good.
You'll know that if Susan goes along with your suggestions, Patrick
will too. And if Edward sees that you haven't been hasty, he may just
go along with what you propose.

As the politically astute know, speaking up before you know how
others in a room think is naive. Many competent people fail to
reach their potential because they can't get this simple fact through
their heads. They convince themselves that their ideas aren't enthu-
siastically adopted because they're surrounded by imbeciles. They

don't realize who the real imbecile is, politically speaking. They may spend days, weeks, and months trying to convince people to adopt an idea solely on its merits, while failing to take into account whose oxen will be gored and who will benefit politically. And then they wonder bitterly why their best ideas never see the light of day or, worse, why somebody else later ran with them and succeeded!

I recently met with an exceptionally intelligent vice-president who should be at least president of his own company by now. After listening to several stories about his impatience with the people he works with, and realizing that this was probably the third meeting we'd had of this kind, I decided to offer a little uninvited coaching.

"Do you ever make people feel good about adopting your ideas?" I asked him.

He looked puzzled. "That's not why they hired me," he replied curtly.

"Oh, but it is. At least in part," I said. "They thought you were one of them. Now they know you're not, because you deliver your ideas in ways that make them look bad." He seemed receptive, so I continued. "In fact, given the sarcasm in your voice when you describe what you say to them, I'd venture to guess that you make them feel inferior."

He reflected on this, then said, "I'm no politician, if that's what you mean."

I nodded. "That may be true. But, then again, it couldn't hurt to try a few strategies, to deliver your ideas in more effective ways. I don't see any downside. The next time someone, even one of the most annoying of your colleagues, has a reasonably good idea, try telling him so. Don't overdo it. Just say, 'I hadn't thought of that,' 'That's an important insight,' or 'I see now what you mean.' "

At first he resisted a bit: "That's not me. I hate flattery."

"This is not obsequious flattery," I offered. "It's merely giving someone who has proposed a good idea a chance to look good. And in so doing, you'll likely find they'll listen more closely to what you have to say."

This same vice-president spends a lot of time wondering why he hasn't been noticed. In actuality he has been noticed but for the wrong reasons. His brilliant ideas tend to fall on deaf ears because no one wants to tell someone who's convinced he's better than everyone else that indeed he's right.

Focus on showing how smart you are when other people are worrying about how you're making them look, and you'll lose every time. But you'll vastly increase your chances of successfully pressing your agenda if you

- Do your political homework.
- Identify the relevant players and their agendas.
- Smooth over the rough spots in advance.
- Identify possible objections and deal with them before they become hardened positions.
- Find ways for other deserving people to get personal credit.

Know Your Strengths and Weaknesses

All the successful people I've interviewed have had a good sense of both what they do well and what they don't do well. When *Fortune* magazine examined why CEOs fail, it identified such factors as per-formance credibility, focus on basic execution, sending too much bad news, board issues, and team discontentment. But at the core of many of these issues is an inability for many hard-charging people to see that no one does everything well. Just as a tiring baseball pitcher often refuses to recognize when it's time to hand the ball over to a relief pitcher, any truly competitive individual has a tendency to think he or she can accomplish something by dint of pure intelligence, guts, and effort. Not so with Steve Delcarson, who as mentioned in chapter 2 has successfully grown several companies not merely by his keen insights and entrepreneurial bent but by recognizing his strengths. His current company provides computer training tailored to specific organizational needs. "I'm better at building than maintaining," Delcarson says. "I like the unknown— a business managing chaos that I can turn from 15 to 50 percent growth."

On route to becoming an All-American gymnast, Delcarson had two different influential coaches. One coach was a methodical planner who required the gymnasts to keep a calendar of daily goals. "If you showed up without it or with nothing written, he sent you away to find something to write," Delcarson explained, amused and appreciative now that he understands fully what that taught him. His second coach "was a driver seven days a week. It was grueling, but he created a gymnast dynasty." Strongly influenced by both a strategic thinker and a hard driver, Delcarson is capable of getting past challenges to achieve what seem to many others unreachable goals.

Every significant organizational project or change process undergoes five stages: planning, enabling, launching, catalyzing, and maintaining. Delcarson likes the planning and enabling aspects of a new venture. He readily admits that maintaining a company isn't his strong suit. It's to your powerful advantage to assess where you fit best in any such project or process. If you're a Commanding type, for example, who always winds up taking on jobs that require a great deal of planning and/or enabling, you're certainly not going to be fully utilizing your strengths. Commanding types without a strong Inspirational backup style are impatient with creative endeavors; those without a strong Supportive backup are impatient with people who don't catch on quickly. They aren't best suited to planning or enabling. All of us have such style-based areas of strengths and weaknesses. The table below shows what kind of leadership it takes to be effective at each point in a project or change effort.[4]

Senior Manager Leadership Styles
for the Five Phases of
Organizational Change

PROJECT PHASE	FOCUS OF ACTIVITIES	APPROPRIATE LEADERSHIP STYLE
Planning	Acquiring information	Logical/Inspirational
	Creating ideas	Inspirational
	Formulating strategy	Logical
Enabling	Explaining plan	Logical
	Convincing employees	Logical
	Empowering/involving	Inspirational/Supportive
	Assisting	Supportive
Launching	Implementing steps	Logical
	Meeting goals	Commanding
	Getting results	Commanding
	Assessing progress	Logical
Catalyzing	Inspiring	Inspirational

	Energizing	Inspirational
	Assisting	Supportive
Maintaining	Overseeing progress	Logical
	Guiding	Inspirational
	Energizing	Inspirational
	Assisting	Supportive
© 1998 by Kathleen Reardon, Kevin Reardon, and Alan Rowe.		

If you've been taking on roles that don't suit your style, you're limiting your chances of achieving the secret handshake. People who achieve the secret handshake know where their greatest strengths lie.

Impeccable Timing

Timing is one of the most difficult skills to teach. It requires astute observation and almost a sixth sense. Just as time has become a competitive advantage for many companies, how you handle time can powerfully impact your own forward progress.

One of my former M.B.A. students who is now a very successful senior executive with a Fortune 500 company says, "In the dot-com era timing is all-important." Waiting too long to let your boss know important information can harm your career. Asking for a promotion or raise when the company is having financial problems may easily be taken as a sign of disloyalty. Bringing up delicate subjects early in a relationship—or even too early in a conversation—can cause offense. Yet the dot-com era has speeded up decisions. What you might have given desk-drawer time to before has to be decided now in minutes. At least that's what we've come to believe.

There's a good chance that while we're grabbing opportunities left and right, we're missing the mark a lot. Jeff Bezos, Amazon.com's CEO, told the *Wall Street Journal* that he pushes people to work faster "even if it means a worse initial product." This is not an uncommon view in fast-moving e-commerce businesses. But it's coming back to haunt some of them. Bezos also says that he takes time to step back, sets aside a fraction of time for his own, and doesn't travel more than a third of the time. He uses Tuesdays and Thursdays to reflect a bit and to say thank you to people. Bezos has recognized that even in the dot-com era, not giving yourself some downtime is a sure way to lose sight of the objectives.[5]

Timing issues come up every day. For example, when should you approach a boss with a complaint? Ken Williams, a high-tech executive based in Washington, D.C., told me that when he was interviewed for his current job, his boss promised him that he'd be included in meetings with the CEO. On that promise he took the job. Later the same boss told him he'd have to renege on that promise. Williams was livid. "I went into his office and told him he'd just made it easy for me to be stolen. If a good offer comes along, I'm gone." On the one hand, he'd gotten his anger off his chest. On the other, rather than use his boss's broken promise as an opportunity to negotiate some other benefit, he'd closed a door. The time to tell your boss that you're leaving is when you *are* leaving, not when you're thinking about it.

Good timing means paying attention to setting and mood as well as to how you express yourself. Don Shellgren, whom I introduced in chapter 3, is a wine aficionado. He has a cellar stocked with some of the most sought-after wines in the world. "One of my former bosses thought he knew everything about restaurants. He had been to the best ones all over the world. But he didn't really know much about wine. He loved Pouilly-Fuissé. It's an okay wine, but if you know your wines, you know it's not great. One night he invited a group of us out. We listened to him go on and on about wine. People hung on his every word. I looked disinterested, maybe disgusted, so he said, 'Don, you don't seem to be thrilled with the food and wine.' I looked at him and said, with obvious disdain for his lowly knowledge of wine and his undeserved superior attitude about it, 'Mr. Clark, I'm not exactly a coyote getting his first taste of chicken.' Showing up the boss like that set my career back five years."

I once watched incredulously as a young woman introduced herself to a pharmaceutical company recruiter visiting our campus. I'd been speaking with him at his booth for a few minutes when the woman interrupted us.

"Excuse me," she said impatiently. "I don't mean to interrupt you two, but is anyone else at this booth?"

The man replied politely, "Yes, the other recruiter will be right back."

He had resumed speaking to me when the woman interrupted again: "I want to leave my résumé."

"Okay," he said, accepting it. "I'll give it to Mary when she gets here."

He turned to me again, and once again the woman interrupted him: "I want to get someone's name so I can follow up."

By this time I was impressed with the recruiter's patience. "By all means," he said. He reached for a piece of paper and wrote down a name and number. It wasn't his. He handed it to the annoyed woman and told her, "Call this person and she'll be glad to let you know what we think. Thank you for stopping by." He turned back to me and she went away.

This woman's impatience and insistence had quite obviously

cost her any chance at a job. Had she been more sensitive to timing, she might be working at that company today.

The Balancing Act

It is critical in business that you balance people concerns with project goals. While many employees struggle to locate the most creative or brilliant solution, people who are politically savvy ask themselves:

- Does my solution respond to senior management's concerns?
- Does it fly in the face of the philosophy of the company?
- Who looks good if we adopt it? Who looks bad?
- Is there a way to reshape it to respond to the needs, desires, and concerns of key people?
- Who can help me assess this situation?

Most people look for a solution that addresses only the immediate problem, and the sooner the better. That's fine if it doesn't unnecessarily disrupt the political landscape in the process. If it creates more obstacles for the people implementing it or those affected by it, however, it's either only half a solution or another problem in the making. You have to think on two tracks when defining a problem and finding a solution. One is to solve the problem. The other, which is equally important, is making sure people involved are not adversely affected by that solution.

Occasionally, a solution is both highly effective in solving the problem and highly effective politically. More often than not, however, there is a trade-off. Since organizations are composed of people, their concerns can't be overlooked without sacrifice. When decision-makers focus exclusively on project issues, as is so often the case, the political trade-offs can have serious negative consequences down the line.

Laura Tyson, former economic adviser to President Clinton and now dean of the Haas School of Business at UC Berkeley, describes herself as an "integrator." She is able to step back, look from various perspectives, notice linkages where others see disparity, and, most difficult of all, bring the people advocating diverse views together to see and appreciate similarities of purpose or principle.

Tyson describes this as "the ability to be direct but yet respectful." She is able to strike a balance between project and people concerns. When people are going down a path she believes to be disadvantageous, she'll reason with them. She might say, "It boils down to this: If you can't do A or B, this won't work. I understand if you can't do A or B, but let's be clear about what that means." Tyson prefers this approach to knocking down barriers or violating the opinions of others to reach goals. Her leadership style is more Logical and Supportive than Commanding. It is what allows her to achieve balance by responding respectfully to disparate views and opposing constituencies.

Tyson sees this skill as a disinclination to go to the mat on things. She prefers to "bring people along" by reasoning through why something should be done. She strikes a balance between their interests and her goals. Is this kind of balanced thinking a weakness? It certainly hasn't hurt Tyson's career. She's the kind of person you want around when you're convincing Congress or a president that the actions being taken are based on sound economic principles. One time when she did go to the mat, she learned that when you do, you'd better be the one with the decision power to carry through. When Hillary Rodham Clinton promoted a national health-care plan, Tyson pushed for her to consider the potential negative ramifications. The press went after Tyson, based on information from detractors implying that she was either naive or in Machiavellian fashion trying to bring down the administration's health-care program. "I learned you can be direct, but you also have to be able to give way," Tyson told me, "especially when you're not the one making the final decision."

Unless you're running the show, you need to find a way to get your thoughts across in a manner palatable to those around you. Find ways to integrate their ideas and yours. Instead of taking sides, take stock of where they stand, where you stand, who stands to win, who to lose, and then try to choose a route that provides a reasonable amount of mutual gain. I can almost hear some people thinking, "Who has time for all that?" The answer: It doesn't take much time once you've practiced. In fact, it saves you a great deal of time since you don't have to deal with the revenge of people who think you walked on them to achieve your goals.

5.

Forming Relationships the Politically Savvy Way

―――――

The next set of political skills important to achieving the secret handshake involves creating the relationships that make it happen. The ineffective execution of this critical aspect of business politics derails careers every day. To become a part of the inner circle, key relationships must be strategically developed and nurtured.

Lining Up Your Ducks

Let's start with a well-known rule of human nature: *People tend to do what's in their best interests.* Political savvy requires knowing what others need and want. "I make myself get up from this desk a few times each day to visit with people," says a successful IBM executive. He does this to learn what is going on and also to keep key people aware of him. "I always go in with something to ask or say of interest, and then I read the situation and decide how long to stay. I got ahead by doing this when other people wouldn't."

Strategic visits to peers and senior people have several advantages. They provide opportunities to let others know of your accomplishments. Sharon Allen, partner with Deloitte & Touche, learned early on the importance of this strategy. "A few years into my twenty-seven-year career here, I was still thinking that all of my great work was being noted and that I'd eventually be fully acknowledged." When that acknowledgment didn't come, Allen sought the advice of a mentor. "He told me that nobody had really noticed all the things I was doing." It came as a surprise to her, but she learned a valuable lesson: "You can't assume that people know what you're doing well. You have to let them know."

Allen knew that loudly touting her accomplishments not only didn't fit her personal style but also wasn't the politically correct way for women in her organization to get ahead. "I touted quietly by mentioning my accomplishments to direct superiors and others above me in one-to-one conversations, rather than in group meetings. I copied letters of compliment to them. Occasionally, I mentioned someone of stature whom I'd worked with on a particular project."

Allen now believes that "people are generally too shy and reticent about putting their achievements in front of important others. They worry too much about how it will sound. So long as you don't stumble into someone's office and say, 'I want to tell you about the impressive things I've done,' you're better off letting them know."

Allen is absolutely right. People are far too busy to follow or be aware of your accomplishments. You have to let them know. The key here is to be strategic in telling them. Choose the right method and time. Few people look forward to a visit from somebody who wanders the halls all day, coffee cup in hand, dropping in and out of people's offices, causing them to interrupt their work.

Another advantage of strategic visits is the opportunities they provide to let people know what you can do for them. When Arlene Falk Withers joined Transamerica as a young attorney, she did just that. "Transamerica didn't know they needed me," Withers told me, but she knew they did. At first, she "floated around" the company's offices and introduced herself to people, always with a good reason for doing so. She lunched with senior managers, learned their interests and current projects. Later on she followed up with strategic visits, asking more probing questions about the senior executives' intended actions on those projects.

Withers describes herself as a "student of people." She's not afraid to ask, 'Why do you think that? Why did you do that? What will happen now?' As she says, "What people ask for often isn't what they need or want; by asking questions you learn more, and then you can use that knowledge to help them be more effective at what they do." In time, Withers developed a store of information she could use to keep senior managers and middle managers and professionals in touch with each other. "I had a good sense of knowing what would be of value to them. My early law firm experience was helpful. It was very service-oriented. You gave people your home phone number and said, 'Call me anytime day or night.' Of course, they didn't, but the gesture was very much appreciated. The same approach worked well at Transamerica too."

Withers taught herself to be a pro at laying the groundwork for the unknown future need. While she admits "the cachet of being a lawyer makes people think you know what you're talking about," she attributes most of her success to her strategic visits. They enabled her to learn what key people needed to successfully implement their projects and to offer ways that she might help them.

Managing Reciprocity

"You scratch my back and I'll scratch yours" may seem a crass philosophy, but it's at the heart of many successful careers. Consider Madeleine Albright's rise from obscurity to become secretary of state. Yes, competence had a lot to do with it, but Albright also made the right connections and laid the political groundwork in advance. She entered the workforce late, at age thirty-nine. Her first full-time job was as chief legislative assistant to Senator Edmund Muskie. It was certainly a good start, but hardly the inner circle. There she kept a fairly low profile, according to *New Yorker* writer Michael Dobbs.[1] She served as congressional liaison for National Security Adviser Zbigniew Brzezinski, who'd been one of her professors at Columbia.

When in 1987 Albright became foreign policy adviser to presidential candidate Michael Dukakis, it got the attention of the Washington political in-group. And when Arkansas Governor Bill Clinton helped prepare Dukakis for his TV debate with George Bush, Albright made Clinton's acquaintance. A year later, Clinton asked her for a letter of recommendation to the Council on Foreign Relations, and she obliged with high praise for the young governor. In 1992, according to Dobbs, President-elect Clinton returned the favor. "When aides presented him with a list of members of the foreign policy transition team, he underlined Albright's name and jotted the word 'good' beside it." Clinton named Albright U.S. ambassador to the United Nations.

Was Albright qualified for the job? Undoubtedly, yes. But were other people also qualified? Most certainly so. A favor had been earned, and returned. Albright later became U.S. secretary of state.

An equally impressive story of politically strategic reciprocity—in this case, the result of discomfort with it—is that of women's rights champion Betty Friedan. *New Yorker* writer Daphne Merion has described Friedan as "a shadowy presence, an icon without portfolio . . . pushed to the sidelines of the very movement she had founded."[2] Here is a woman who presided over the rebirth of feminism in the early 1960s after writing the bestseller *The Feminine Mystique,* and who shortly thereafter cofounded the National Organization for Women (NOW). Friedan fought passionately for equal pay and equal rights, but her place in history may have been jeopardized by what biographer Judith Hennessee called her "breathtaking incivility for which she was fiercely resented."[3] By this account, Friedan's quickness to anger deprived her of richly deserved honors received by many lesser contributors to women's rights.

Friedan and I team-taught together at the Marshall School of Business and hosted senior executive conferences for the Leadership Institute. Yes, she was quick to anger and even raised her voice in anger at me in public, but on those rare occasions I would stand up and give her the same right back. Apparently, this was something Friedan was not used to, and she would whisper at me, "Sit down, sit down! I'm not yelling—in New York we talk that way!" Despite these occasions, Friedan was often wonderfully warm and a wellspring of knowledge and wisdom. I learned a great deal from her and I saw many others do the same.

People wanted to meet her no matter where we went. In restaurants they'd come up and say, "You changed my life." She would usually smile, nod briefly, and continue with our conversation. At receptions where people in power came up to meet her, she often did the same. I watched Friedan miss or avoid opportunities to chat with people who could have been quite helpful to her. Yet, to her credit, she would spend untold hours with students who had little to offer beyond their interest.

It isn't in Friedan's nature to play political games. Otherwise she would have glad-handed many a night away with all sorts of pompous and impossible people. Betty grew tired of that very quickly, and it was easy for her to snap at a remark that cut at the heart of an issue she cared about. She seemed to have no time to educate the ignorant. They annoyed her, and it didn't matter whether they'd done her a favor or not.

"I've never been good at the social graces," Friedan explained to me. "And I've never had a political strategy." For her the issue has always been paramount. As she says of herself in her book *Life So Far*, "I always could count on my mind."[4] Time will tell whether this unwillingness to schmooze will be held against Friedan. "I have no complaints about how I've been treated," she says. "I've been fortunate enough to have been heard."

Not many people can be as successful at being heard as Friedan in the absence of advanced social graces. Asking someone you've never bothered to establish a relationship with for a favor or believing she'll think of you when a promotion opportunity arises is a form of political fumbling. She doesn't know whether you'll ever return the favor since she doesn't know your track record. She doesn't owe you anything and hasn't the foggiest idea what you'll ever be able to do for her. If you want to be remembered come promotion time, you need to have established a support base of people for whom you've done some impressive work or favors.

Developing Your Favor Bank

Many people damage their careers by not realizing that they have favors to give. Everyone has the ability to do favors. First you need to take stock of how you can be helpful. Think of yourself as the owner of a favor bank that you can fill with ways to be an asset to others. Here are some examples of favors that might be in your bank right now ready to be given:

- Your boss is a collector of some hard-to-find items and you know where to find some at good prices.
- A colleague is late with a project and you can help expedite things.
- A boss looks pressured, so you stay late to give him some help.
- Your boss is being pulled in a lot of directions and you compliment him on managing it all.
- You are proficient at a word-processing program used by a key person, so when you see him or her pounding on the computer, you provide a brief overview of how it works.
- You know of a task that ties up a lot of a superior's time. You share with him or her a way to cut that time in half.

It wouldn't hurt to take a few minutes right now to assess the contents of your favor bank. How can someone use your help, attention, expertise, or encouragement? Politically adept people think this way. They know what they have to offer.

Giving isn't all just to make people think well of you. It has some additional redeeming features. Los Angeles County Sheriff's Department Chief of Detectives Elizabeth Dickinson is an avid mentor. "One of my greatest rewards," she says, "is seeing people I've mentored do so for others." This attitude has not only advanced the careers of many young officers but has won Dickinson the respect of colleagues at every level of the Sheriff's Department. Add to this her disdain for selfish advancement moves and it's little wonder that she was chosen as chief: "I've always shared acknowledgment of those below, next to, and above me." From all reports, this respect Dickinson shows to others has been given back to her three-fold.

In giving and receiving favors, it's important to remember that reciprocity applies to appreciation too. I once helped a friend and colleague land a new job after she'd been fired due to style differences with her boss. After she'd taken the job she stopped calling me. I remember telling myself that a lot of people do this, but while I'd done the favor out of personal concern for her and with no expectation of a material return, the absence of even a "thank you" coupled with her ending the relationship was offensive to me. A mutual friend who had the same experience with her told me, "She is one of those people who use and move on." This kind of neglect or ingratitude is not advisable. People who, as a rule, take and forget are not destined for the secret handshake—at least not for long.

It's also important not to overdo things with reciprocity or, indeed, any political tactic. Ben Franklin was absolutely right: "Everything in moderation." If you do too many things for people too often, favors cease to have significance, or may even become off-putting. And what you do for people should be something they cannot otherwise easily obtain, although it can be as simple as a ride home if their car breaks down.

The Power of Unexpected Favors

Timing is key here as well. Unexpected favors can be very powerful. One executive told me how she had years earlier helped some other middle managers then at her level by providing them with copies of two of the six systems engineering exams she'd taken. One of these managers later became her boss. Because of this unexpected favor she provided him when she had nothing obvious to gain, he recently ordered all the books and materials she needs for the remainder of her exams.

Another surprise that makes an impact is a thank-you note. It's a form of etiquette that has become infrequent. That is why it is impressive. If a person did you a favor by meeting with you, an immediate thank-you note is effective. If, however, the person has only spoken with you in passing, the impact of a personal note recalling something he said might be greater if you send it a month after you met. That you remember his interests so long after parting company indicates that you were really listening to him and that he's remained on your mind.

Knowing How Long You Owe Them

Sometimes a thank-you note is a far cry from what is owed. When someone saves you from being fired or helps get you your dream position, the debt is long-term. This is the case even if this person says you don't owe her a thing. Just how long you do owe her is one of the secrets that must be uncovered if you want to make it to the inner circle.

One of the most common errors in the back-and-forth of favors is insufficient gratitude. For large favors, gratitude for a lifetime might be in order. When that person calls on you for assistance, you provide it. This doesn't mean you lose all integrity and reciprocate in whatever fashion desired by the favor donor. Hopefully, he or she won't expect that of you. It does mean that unless an opportunity comes along that allows you to pay back the favor with one at least as great as the one you received, the obligation continues.

The reason for this unstated obligation is that society is built around give-and-take. Without it we'd probably all be selfish brutes. It's a two-edged sword, however, since the joy of receiving in business often brings with it an obligation to the donor that may live on for years or decades. If you can't play this game, you might as well give up the secret handshake right now. Indeed, there are times when businesspeople help others out of sheer altruism, but even in those rare cases reciprocated respect and regard are expected. Fail to provide it, and the Good Samaritan may become your enemy.

How do you know the length of time or amount of reciprocity required? By observing. Unless you've received a favor from an anonymous donor, people around you are likely to mention the lengths to which a certain person went to help you. They'll imply or state that you owe this person. After a while, you'll be able to gauge what constitutes a big favor and you'll know how to respond.

When I was facing a difficult promotion, one colleague of mine put himself in particular jeopardy to help me scale a very high obstacle. He challenged a superior who stood in my path and garnered assistance from others with clout. I owe him to this day. Another time a very well-established colleague informed me of a potential obstacle to promotion. He also took visible steps to help me clear the path, even recommending the removal from the selection committee of a person who'd expressed opposition to my promotion. After I received the promotion, a colleague said to me, "Wow, you sure owe him big-time. You'll need to vote his way for a long while, nod when he talks, and be there for any job he sees fit to call you for." This may have been a bit of an exaggeration, but it was a clear articulation of the rule of reciprocity. Were I to violate it in any overt fashion, not only would the generous colleague be shocked but so, too, would those aware of what he'd done.

The next time someone does you a favor, be sure to assess what it took for them to do so and what you can do in return. Whatever you do, don't forget their contribution. Occasionally mention your gratitude, compliment them at an important moment, support them in an endeavor important to them, or be there when they need someone to run interference. Don't be too obvious about it. You'll embarrass the donor. If you must disagree with them publicly, do so by delicately prefacing your comments with praise for their view and positioning yours as a related alternative. The person who does this well is admired by the one owed as well as those who may someday be of help.

There are times, however, when someone expects too much in return. Roy Romer, former governor of Colorado and chair of the Democratic National Committee and now the superintendent of the Los Angeles Unified School District, told me, "You can't allow people to influence you to do what you shouldn't. You should take their phone calls, though." When he takes those calls, he doesn't let people think they're going to get a favor that simply won't be forthcoming. "I tell people when I can't help and why. I don't lead them on." But Romer will also tell you that he remembers people in other ways. He learns their names and returns favors within limits. Early in his career, he had photos taken of everyone at the Democratic Convention, so he would be able to study their faces and remember their names the next year. He believes, though, that there's a thin line between such harmless politics and manipulation. His advice: "Constantly recognize the evils in letting it go too far."

Give Credit Even When It Isn't Due

The politically astute are not arrogant. They seek advice because they know there are many perspectives from which any situation can be viewed. They know, too, that people selectively perceive, and so they never get the whole picture from one source. And perhaps most important, they know that giving someone a chance to be an expert is a favor in itself. It subtly applies the rule of reciprocity. Give others opportunities to feel intelligent, clever, witty, or creative, and they'll likely return the favor.

Lieutenant General Claudia Kennedy, U.S. Army deputy chief of staff for intelligence, is the highest-ranking woman in the U.S. Army. She reached the inner circle as a three-star general in part because she sought and listened to advice and steered clear of making people look bad. Kennedy experienced a significant assignment disappointment early in her career. "I was told that I was slated to get a premier battalion but ultimately I didn't get it. Later, I found out that someone had worked his way around the system." Kennedy let her superiors know of her disappointment, but she stopped short of taking further steps. "It's generally not a good idea to respond with threats," Kennedy said. "You don't reestablish authority; you only relieve emotions. You need to assume that another door will open. They always do." Kennedy describes her philosophy as, "Don't go too far. Make your point to the person who can change things and then get on with your business." She doesn't shirk from being a "burr under the saddle" when need be, but she doesn't push superiors until they do things her way. She makes her point firmly. "I'm loyal. They know that. I focus on 'we the army.' If they don't do what I'm recommending, at least they've heard me and they'll benefit from that the next time a similar situation comes up."

Kennedy is able to keep her dealings with her superiors rational rather than personal because she is very comfortable with her commitment and direction. "I was taught that I am the ultimate judge of myself. I'm sensitive to what others tell me. I learn from advice. I don't take the negative messages too personally."

Kennedy also advises, "Never lock yourself into a position. Leave yourself room. Remain agile until you find out where they're coming from." She recommends not pointing out "that an underlying belief a superior has is wrong, because he or she will spend valuable time defending it." Instead, she prefers to show people with whom she disagrees how the particular case under discussion does not fit the category in which they've placed it. This is much less threatening, doesn't seem arrogant, and gives the other person the opportunity to retain his or her philosophy while perhaps seeing that you may have a point.

"I challenged some sacred cows when I was younger," Kennedy told me. "But now I persuade and find what counts to the other person. Then I try to bring him to my way of thinking." Kennedy doesn't consider it important that she get all the credit for her sug-

gestions. She's observed that the top brass in the military, like business senior executives, prefer to "do things they think are their own
ideas."

There's a skill of patiently bringing people to your way of thinking even when you'd like to say, "You're absolutely wrong" or
"That's one of the most ridiculous comments I've ever heard." A
more astute approach is to ask some questions. Get more information. Then use connective comments such as these to link your idea
to that of the other person:

- "I see now what you're saying. I hadn't thought of it that
  way. There's an additional consideration I'd like to pose that
  goes to the heart of what you're looking for here."
- "Given that position, we might want to consider making a
  slight alteration in the plan. It fits well with what you said
  earlier about . . ."
- "That really helped clarify things. I see now why you've
  gone in the direction you have. It seems reasonable then to
  consider doing X, which fits well with the direction you've
  outlined here."

Only desperate people grab all the credit. And they appear desperate when they do so. Most of the time even people who are
wrong have a rationale for what they're doing. The politically adept
seek to understand that rationale. They express agreement with
whatever part they honestly can and then use that similarity of
thinking as a bridge to their own suggestions.

Such comments as "I'd like to hear what you're thinking, Alex,"
"You're the expert in this area, Ellen, what's your opinion?" and

"Sam, since you handled a delicate situation like this not long ago, can you give us the benefit of your expertise?" do wonders to discourage others from resisting your ideas.

It's important to sincerely believe what you're saying, or the compliment will seem contrived. If you recognize, as General Kennedy does, that people have their reasons for doing things and it's your job to discover what they are, you'll make a lot fewer enemies and many more high-placed friends.

Making Connections

Some people are great collectors of influential acquaintances. On the other hand, I've attended conferences, especially those designed and attended primarily by women, where everyone has been encouraged to share business cards and spend the day finding people with whom to network. People would go from table to table tossing their cards to whoever seemed important.

This is a case of a good political strategy being seriously misapplied. The more sophisticated organizational politicians don't haphazardly fling their cards at complete strangers. In fact, they seem to have a kind of radar that tells them whom they should seek out. This radar comes from having done their homework. Before conferences and dinners, they find out who will be attending, and by the time the conference starts they know whom they'll try to arrange or "strategically chance" to meet. A true mover and shaker works the room—any room—intelligently. While others are spinning their wheels, they're zeroing in on those they need to attract to their web of relationships.

The "who you know" rule only works when the emphasis is on the word *"know."* It is *not* the "who you meet" rule. It's one thing to have met someone in passing, and another thing entirely to actually know that person. In the latter case, a relationship has been established—even if it's a relatively new one.

Horace Deets, executive director of the 34 million-member American Association of Retired Persons, has access to many influential people on Capitol Hill. But Deets says such access is effective only to the extent that the people you're accessing consider you reliable, consistent and professional. "I'm not interested in photo ops with celebrities," Deets told me of his relationships with people like senators James Jeffords and Ted Kennedy. "That's okay for cocktail party bragging rights but it doesn't accomplish things."

According to Deets, it's one thing to have met someone in passing, and another thing entirely to actually know them. In the latter case, a relationship has been established. "You learn things about people when you really get to know them," Deets told me. His first impression of Newt Gingrich is a case in point. "I thought he would be impossible to work with and I believe he thought the same of me. But we got to know each other," Deets explains, "and I've done a complete 180-degree turn on what I think of him. I believe he's done the same regarding me and AARP." Deets believes that making valuable connections involves conveying to others a sense of having truly noticed and listened to them. When I talked with Deets, *Fortune* magazine had ranked AARP the strongest lobby in Washington, D.C., for three consecutive years. "Really knowing people assures that you'll get a fair hearing," Deets says of AARP's lobbying effectiveness. "You can't coerce members of Congress. We're responsive to their interests, explain our positions reasonably, and never try to ridicule them, so they listen to the merits of our proposals."

Making valuable connections involves conveying to others a sense of having truly noticed them. Eye contact helps achieve this, especially if coupled with a firm handshake. Politically adept people find something intriguing about each person they meet. Ciara Egan, IT manager with SmithKline Beecham, describes it this way: "My favorite thing is to study people. I'm always looking around. I try not to miss a trick." With the ones potentially helpful to them in the future, the politically savvy are especially attentive. They ask questions of them, seek elaboration of their comments, identify mutual interests about which they can comfortably converse, and express a good reason why they should share business cards to enable future interactions.

Connecting via a Back Door

Getting to know people who can be helpful to your career can be difficult if you don't know how to put yourself in contact with them. Often this takes some creativity.

Imagine a house—let's call it the House of Opportunity. Most people try to gain entry by knocking on the front door and ringing the bell. Far too many ring the doorbell a couple of times, knock on the door, and give up. The more persistent call out, "Is anybody home?," and then leave when there's no answer. But every house has other ways to gain entry: the back door, the windows, the cellar door, skylights, even the chimney. It just takes a little imagination and a willingness to enter a desirable location in an unorthodox manner.

Did you know that Disney CEO Michael Eisner got his start as an usher at NBC in New York? He had tried writing plays, had gone to Paris to become another Ernest Hemingway, had stayed only a week and then come home. He'd tried one job after another in the area of creating ideas. After much trial and error, he found a doorway:

"Since I liked being with people, I became a clerk at NBC. I wrote what time the commercials came on the air. I did traffic for NBC Radio . . . went to CBS, put the commercials in the children's programs, saw every children's program for a couple of years, worked on *The Ed Sullivan Show.* Wrote about three hundred letters trying to get a job anywhere, finally got the job at ABC. And I think when I was about twenty-seven, became in charge of daylight television at ABC having never seen a soap opera in my life . . . I always went into an area that was in last place, with a philosophy, 'You can't fall off the floor.' "[5]

When I interviewed Barry Munitz, president and CEO of the J. Paul Getty Trust, at his office high in the billion-dollar Brentwood Center overlooking Los Angeles, it was clear that like Eisner he also sees entryways invisible to others. But he told me that those stories about executives finding an "in" through the mailroom are reserved for Hollywood and rare there as well. Most people need to find a rabbi, Munitz said, "Someone who'll look after you, smooth your edges, reach out and help you grow." Munitz's secret for doing this well over the years is this: "Capture their attention, listen carefully, learn what they have to offer, and then deliver."

Not born with easy access to success, Munitz has made a point of reacting positively to people in positions to mentor him. Each major move in his career has been facilitated by a bridge provided by others, who saw in him considerable potential, and Munitz made sure their support was not wasted. "They place some of their reputation in your success, and so you have to be sure to come through." There's an obligation that comes with being mentored. You owe the person even if he never says so. The best way to pay them back, Munitz says, is "through performance and contribution."

If you seem to be currying favor, then the kinds of assistance Munitz received often don't happen. "The worst way to seek assistance is to be desperate. You're not going to rescue the boss's daughter from the railroad tracks. To get noticed you have to do important things well. Then when interested people open the door for you, it's important to be aware of it and to jump through." When I asked Munitz for an example, he described how he got the attention of one of his earliest mentors by mentioning that he'd worked for a congressman from President Roosevelt's former home district while he was a literature graduate student at Princeton. "That caught his attention. He was interested."

One of Munitz's staunch supporters is Sherry Lansing, chairwoman of Paramount Studios. When his candidacy for chancellor at the California State University system met with political resistance, it was Lansing who made some important phone calls. "We've been like brother and sister for years," Munitz told me. Their relationship got its start in 1984 when Lansing's mother was ill with cancer. At that time, Munitz was raising money for the M.D. Anderson Cancer Center. A mutual friend brought them together in the hope that Munitz could point Lansing in the right direction to assure that her mother would get the best possible care. After Lansing's mother passed away, Sherry went to Houston to support cancer research. She and Munitz were brought together again. "We hit it off," Munitz said. "Every year our families spend Thanksgiving together."

Barry Munitz's life is a story of extraordinary competence and connections. He has a Midas touch of sorts when it comes to creating effective networks with people in high places. Now he sits atop one of the highest himself, assisting others to achieve similar success.

Play It Close to the Vest

After suggesting ways to nurture valuable relationships at work, I'm now going to add a caveat. You have to know whom to trust with information. Friendship complicates things because it brings with it certain obligations to share information. That's what friends do. They share. So the fewer you have of them at work, the less you'll be pressured to spill the beans when you should be keeping information to yourself.

Munitz distinguishes between types of work relationships. "There are friends, mentors, and a third group composed of sounding boards, networks, and reference points. The higher you go in an organization, the harder it is to make close personal friends because you're in charge. You can't easily confide in or confess inadequacies to someone who works for you." Yet Munitz points out that you can't be a loner either. "It's very important in the leadership center to not get isolated." So while close personal friendships aren't advisable at higher levels, sounding boards and reference points are imperative. You need to be close enough to people for them to keep you in the loop.

Some people are proficient at gleaning information from others without incurring obligation. One method for doing so is *apparent* self-disclosure. A person acts as though she is providing confidential or personal information to another, when in actuality she isn't revealing anything that couldn't be learned with a little effort. The way the information is conveyed, however, implies that it is private and shared only with friends. For example, the person appearing to disclose might whisper or suggest meeting behind closed doors. When this happens, the information recipient feels obligated to reciprocate. So by feigning closeness and self-disclosure, people can elicit information from you. If you want to make it into the inner circle, you can't allow yourself to be so easily duped.

6.

Reading Between
the Lines

———■———

If effective political moves expedite career progress, why are so many people bereft of political sophistication? One reason, pointed out by David Carpenter, chairman and CEO of UniHealth and former chairman, president, and CEO of Transamerica Life Companies, is that management is an art and politics even more so. "Think of one of the greatest artists alive today," Carpenter says. "Let's say we study all he does from morning till night. He drinks orange juice, goes for a run, sits and thinks, skips lunch, and paints only at night. Then we do exactly as he does and we're still not as good as he is. Why? Because what he's doing is art—complex art at that." No amount of mimicking can capture all the skills and talent that the most accomplished artists possess. They have, aside from that set, an additional ingredient—what Carpenter refers to as "high intuitive powers."

Do we throw up our hands in despair? Just because most of us will never be a Michelangelo of business politics doesn't mean we should give up. Most of us have sufficient intuitive powers to reach a high level of political sophistication. All of us are capable of improving upon the level we're at. What keeps us back, in part, is the sparse amount of time and effort devoted to teaching both children *and* adults how to read between the lines. For many people, it seems to be somehow unethical to foster political awareness early in life. When I hear this "spare the youth" perspective, I'm reminded of what Aristotle said to Plato when that great Greek educator insisted that common people should never be allowed to learn persuasive techniques. Plato insisted that since persuasion could be used for evil ends, training in its tactics should be restricted to people who were ethically righteous by virtue of their privileged education and upbringing. Wrong, argued Aristotle. If you don't teach people how persuasion takes place, they will become unwitting victims of any unscrupulous persons who do have such knowledge.

I'm with Aristotle. The same can be said of business and personal politics as was said of Greek society thousands of years ago: *If people are kept in the dark, they will be at the mercy of those who have not been so deprived.* The key is to learn some political strategies, ones that go beyond the tactics for establishing relationships described in chapter 5.

Improving Your Powers of Observation

The first on the list of key strategies needed for political sophistication is improving your powers of observation. Most people know that listening is crucial to effective business; in fact, this topic is one of my most requested business training sessions. But listening for informational or emotional content isn't enough. Effective listening means not just hearing what your boss or peer said and the tone he or she used to say it but determining what he or she really *meant* as well.

Much of each day people engage in inference. We draw conclusions from incomplete information. We communicate by hint and innuendo in order to keep people from actually figuring out what we mean and then are surprised when they judge us as self-serving, jealous, demeaning, etc. Erving Goffman calls this evasiveness "tact": the ability to say things in ways that allow us to avoid having to take responsibility for what was said should it go awry. Tact is being able to say what you mean in a way that is deniable.[1]

Here's an example. The CEO of a large financial firm was displeased with the performance of his chief operations officer. Rather than engage in a confrontation, the CEO opted for something subtler. When he was invited to speak to a professional association of COOs, instead of asking his COO for advice on the speech, he wrote the text entirely himself. In the body of the speech, he enumerated all the things an effective COO should do for his CEO and his company. Many of these were things that his own COO either wasn't doing very well or wasn't doing at all. The CEO then sent the speech to the COO for "input." Subtextual message: *"If you plan to stick around, you'd better get with the program and become this kind of COO."* The COO returned the text of the speech with only one comment: "I got your message." Subtextual message: *"You want me out of here? All right, then, I'm gone."* And within a few months the COO indeed was gone.

Messages of dismissal can be sent by merely refusing to give someone the same amount of eye contact that is given to others during a meeting. I was asked by a CEO to observe the dynamics of meetings at his fast-growing entrepreneurial venture. He was concerned about communication, his own included. While observing I noticed how he let a direct report know that her work had not met his standards. He visually canvassed the room, pausing to look momentarily at each person. Each one except her, that is. This continued for the entire meeting. When she did speak up, he abruptly moved on to another topic as if she hadn't said anything at all. I later learned that since he often did this kind of thing to people with whom he was displeased, it was a message she had learned to read. Rather than say, "Your profits are down and you need to get your division back on track," he simply looked past the offending person, making her, in his eyes, "nonexistent." Others at the table got the message—"I'm not pleased with her so don't you talk to her either." And they didn't.

Another CEO holds a birthday party each year. He makes sure to have his picture taken with each guest as a memento of the occasion. At a meeting just prior to the party, one of his direct reports had openly disagreed with him about an important issue. When this manager arrived at the party, the CEO turned away from the photo opportunity and walked into the adjacent room. The manager knew instantly he was in trouble. That year his photo would not be in the album. And if things didn't change soon, he would never be in it again.

People who can't read these subtle and not-so-subtle messages don't last long at companies. They keep making the same mistakes. I worked with a newly promoted sales manager who had this problem. She interpreted everything verbatim. Subtlety was not her strong suit. Yet she was very talented at sales, and her clients were devoted. Teaching her to read between the lines was akin to moving a child from concrete to abstract thinking in five easy lessons. It wasn't going to happen. Although she learned a lot and became much more observant, which pleased her boss, the culture of her company was highly political, and she was not destined to succeed in such a milieu. Yet she could be very successful in a minimally or moderately politicized culture, especially with the work we put into tweaking her style. Eventually, she realized that and moved on to where her talents could be better appreciated.

While a lot of negative messages are sent subtly, so are many positive ones. It's important to be able to tell when you're being sent a message of encouragement. The politics of compliment is often as subtle as the politics of disdain. Since favoritism is seen as unfair in many cultures, giving someone an opportunity or advancing him or her past others who are equally or more qualified is often done quietly behind the scenes. But you need to be able to detect when someone is covertly extending a helping hand.

"She's never happy, no matter what I do." This is how a senior executive I was coaching described one of his direct reports. "I give her a compliment and she doesn't even notice. When she does notice, she always looks for an ulterior motive. There's no pleasing her, so I've stopped trying." He was right. The dynamics were just as he described them. This woman was incapable of seeing that her new boss was trying to compliment her. She'd brought to this new relationship so much "baggage" from the prior one that she couldn't see his good intentions. Defensiveness had become her modus operandi.

To turn things around, I coached her boss in ways to let her know that times had changed, that she could let her defenses down and recognize that he was indeed complimenting her. She had to be encouraged to see that she'd let herself become habitually negative.

Perhaps she had good reason to do so. The prior boss had been a dolt. But she was in a new game now, and playing by old rules was soon going to make her a loser. Once each of them noticed how they'd contributed to the negative outcome of their interactions, they were able to turn things around.

I've observed countless numbers of people miss good news. They're so busy worrying about when the ax will fall that they don't notice when subtle pats on the back are extended in their direction. This is just as dangerous as not seeing subtle negative messages. If you're attuned only to the negative, work becomes joyless. So it's important to notice how compliments are given in your organization. A kind word, a slight pat on the back, a nod, placement on a "hot" project team are a few examples of how some organizations praise people.

In some organizations praise is so obvious and frequent that it is difficult to know when you've been complimented. I worked with one organization where praise had gotten out of hand. "Awesome," "wow," "terrific," and "wonderful" were used even for the most mundane contribution. If a boss told you, "Good work," you'd been insulted.

The intention that leads to this addiction to hyperbole is usually quite admirable. The senior executives want people to feel good about their work. Over time, they increase the intensity of compliments until only the upper end of the praise continuum is utilized. We put a stop to it by bringing the habit to everyone's attention. They laughed when they realized how used to hyperbole they'd become. They decided to widen the praise options and practice until hyperbole had vanished.

When you can't change the culture, however, you have to find ways to deal with it. It's important to notice when you've been complimented even if it's ridiculously overstated. Keep a record of such praise, especially when it comes from people whose opinion is valued. Write thank-you e-mails to those who compliment you and keep copies for your file. There may come a time when you'll need to demonstrate that you've been appreciated. It pays to be ready.

Who's in the Loop and Who's Not?

At a motivation workshop I was conducting, a CEO asked a group of his employees if they believed the messages from senior management were getting out. One brave soul smiled and said, "What messages?" Everyone laughed, but another person added, "Some managers tell their people things we never hear. In fact, sometimes I think no one is supposed to hear some of these things. But clearly, some people are being given the benefit of information a lot of us don't get." This is one of the ways certain people are given a political helping hand—by getting crucial messages others don't.

You need to put yourself in a position to get important information. There are ways to get at least reasonably networked so that you aren't always getting the news when it's no longer new. One common practice by more sophisticated politicians is post-meeting analyses. These often take place by telephone after work hours so others are not suspect of their purpose. "I just called you to see what you thought of today's meeting," some might begin. One very sophisticated secret handshake winner does this regularly. He might say, "I thought of you first because you're so adept at reading between the lines." From there he proceeds to get not only the other person's perceptions of the meeting but also his understanding of what led up to specific events under scrutiny. Who is angry with whom? Who is in favor and who is out of favor? Why is a particular topic getting attention at this time, and what does that mean in terms of future division or organization-wide initiatives? What vested interests were served, which ones overlooked?

Such post-meeting analyses, if not overdone, are vital sources of valuable information. If you aren't already initiating such discussions, it's time to start. Instead of sitting at home in the evening wondering what was meant by a backhand remark directed at you or why two people refused to cooperate with each other and therefore blocked your proposal, pick up the phone and call someone who is in a position to know. "I just wanted to run this by you to get your impression" is a good start. So, too, is, "I was sitting here this evening reflecting on what happened at the meeting this afternoon and I have to admit I'm confused." If you want to read between the lines, it helps to seek the opinions of others who are already experts at it. It's amazing what you'll learn.

Getting Past Access Protection Tactics

In his book *Relations in Public,* sociologist Erving Goffman describes how in status-oriented cultures, people who don't meet certain criteria for group membership are denied access by those who do.[2] Cultural rules for commingling keep the out-group people at a distance without having to tell them they aren't welcome. Even in cultures where equality is valued, access to those with considerable wealth or status is typically denied to persons without such means. Because these norms for commingling exist, there's no need for the well-heeled to wear signs stating: PEOPLE OF MEAGER MEANS OR LOW STATUS SHOULD NOT APPROACH ME. It's just understood by everyone that this is the case. When movie stars are approached in Hollywood by fans, they typically exhibit civility but rarely let down their guard. Smiling as they sign an autograph or engage in a little small talk, they expect that fans will adhere to the notion peculiar to Southern California that "one keeps one's distance from celebrities." Much as these fans might like to invite a star to dinner, they know better.

Organizations have commingling rules as well. Some are made quite clear, as in the case of CEOs who take a private elevator to their offices, leaving no doubt that they wish to be left alone. There's no sign that explicitly states: ONLY THE CEO RIDES THIS ELEVATOR, but the people who work at these companies know that is the case. In most companies there are unwritten rules about who should invite whom to lunch and what styles of dress should be worn. With the emotional distance afforded a management consultant, I'm often able to see these subtle messages more easily than the people working in the organization who are actually sending and receiving them. The conventions become so embedded in the company culture that few people even notice them, much less question them.

In one company where there is supposedly no dress code, the senior managers (all male) wear ties. No one else in the facility wears a tie. This simple, unstated rule conveys status differentiation, which, in turn, implies behavioral parameters. The tie-guys are a breed apart. "I wear ties because I like them," a defensive senior manager told a supervisor who mentioned that he'd noticed the "tie differentiation" in rank at the supposed no-dress-code company. The senior manager denied any intent to convey status. But in a company where team orientation is espoused—where ideas are supposed to be shared by all—the tie convention was very effective in holding out-group people at arm's length, enabling the elect to keep the upper hand and keep the inner circle closed.

Check Your Assumptions at the Door

The largest roadblock in efforts to uncover unstated or unwritten rules and accurately read between the lines is the tendency most of us have to form quick assumptions. Most of us also have an unfortunate tendency to avoid using as much of our brainpower as we can. Researchers actually refer to us humans as "lazy information processors" or "cognitive misers."[3] When we encounter a situation or person that looks similar to others we've experienced before, many of us jump to the conclusion that it's *identical.* The wiser among us are more paced in this attribution process. They may assign a temporary label but will then observe the person or situation for some time before assigning a more enduring one.

Every attribution we make is associated with others of its ilk as we formulate a mini-personality theory whenever we meet someone.[4] If, for example, you meet someone who strikes you as being friendly, you may immediately assign to him attributes that you associate with friendly people, such as funny, happy, reliable, charming, trustworthy, and so forth. When we see people behave in certain ways—in a friendly, disagreeable, cranky, or what seems to be a glad-handing way—there's a tendency to fit those behaviors into stereotypical categories: "She's cooperative," "He's going to be trouble," "She's a bitch," "There's a smooth character," and so forth.

One of the most entrapping assumptions we "lazy" humans

make is to believe that what matters to us must also matter, in the same way and degree, to others. My research on international business gift customs reveals that people who select gifts to give during cross-cultural negotiations based on their own tastes and cultural rules often put those negotiations in considerable jeopardy.[5] Give a clock in China, and you may terminate the business relationship. Present four golf balls or any other item in quadruplet to your Japanese counterpart, and he may wonder why you know so little about his culture. And we don't need to leave our countries to make such mistakes. In all matters of business, egocentric assumptions can easily get in the way of your ability to correctly assess a situation so that you can formulate meaningful, intelligent, and politically effective input.

An indignant engineer once confided in me that his boss had placed far more of a work burden on him than on his peers. He'd confronted the manager, describing the situation as "unfair." The manager had responded, "I'll look into it," but never did. What the engineer had failed to grasp is that *fairness* wasn't a salient issue in a manager's mind—or at least not the primary one. An "unfair" boss may actually see himself as being fair on some other dimension than the one you have in mind. In his or her mind, it may be "fair" to ask one person to do more work because another employee had shouldered the greater burden at an earlier time. If resources are constrained, the manager may find that in order to be "fair" to one person, others must suffer a larger workload or receive lesser rewards. Or perhaps being "unfair" simply accrues to the manager some personal benefit that may not be readily apparent to you. If she shortchanges one person, she may be able to use those resources to influence people who may stand her in good stead. Codes of conduct publicly espoused by senior management are not always the ones that get rewarded. Even in companies that do advocate fairness the real rewards may come from being selectively fair.

If you don't know what motivates someone's behavior—and how to link the things he or she values to those that you need—you've no hope of influencing, managing, or changing the situation. The need to question your assumptions and search for deeper reasons for others' behavior is at the heart of successful business politics.

The politically astute don't assume—they assess. They read each significant situation in terms of the benefits to those involved. They nurture a healthy skepticism regarding easy answers, and choose instead to study human nature. They are not casual observers; they are *professional* observers. For them, getting ahead isn't merely a matter of patience and persistence (although these traits are crucial), and it isn't simply competence that sets them apart, because more often than not, the people around them have comparable skills. The deeper secret, the one you need to know to attain the secret handshake, lies in discovering the importance of suspending your assumptions, examining each situation, looking for the less-than-obvious facts and motivations, and avoiding the fatal slip where you believe that what you see is what you get. Because, more often than not, it just plain isn't so.

Seeing the Disconnects

The skill politically adept people have that allows them to read between the lines is an uncanny ability to detect disconnects between nonverbal and verbal comments. A slight sneer, a snicker, a twitch of the eyes, a turning away, an odd tone of voice, tells them something isn't right. When what is said is not said in the way it should be if it were backed by conviction and complete honesty, people who read between the lines notice.

Ann Lewis, introduced earlier, will tell you that whether you're in Washington, D.C., or anywhere else, "there's a formal set of rules and an informal set. You need to learn the informal set or you're only playing on half the court." It's important to watch and listen— to determine "if what you see is different from what you've been told."

If you're not good at this yet, start with identifying disconnects. The next time someone complains to you, listen past the words to the meaning. Meaning exists on two levels: content and relational.[6] The content meaning is what is said about the subject; the relational meaning is how the person feels about it. If you only listen to content, you get half the message. If you only attend to the emotional expressions—the relational—you get the other half. To get the whole message, you have to hear both. When the two levels don't coincide, that often indicates that the message being sent is complex. A misplaced nod, insufficient eye contact, a slight smirk, or a furrowed brow tells an astute observer that what is being said is likely not what the person is really thinking.

The COO of one of the fastest-growing dot-com companies in the United States has taught herself to assess the CEO's mood before proposing an idea by looking for disconnects. Even if he says he wants the "straight scoop," she knows from observing his demeanor whether he really does. "Our CEO is the typical creative, brilliant entrepreneur who can also be reactive emotionally. When he is emotional, I just nod and say 'Uh-huh' while he's talking."

Even if the CEO says he wants the whole story about a situation, this COO knows not to give it to him if the emotional messages conflict with the content of what he's saying. "If he's angry, I let him rant and rave. I go away and come back later. But I have to be careful. The last time I went back too early. He seemed ready to hear what I had to say, but he wasn't. He accused me of taking something that was black and white and making it gray. He insisted that he'd made clear to me that his decision had been final. He hadn't. But that time I'd failed to deliver my message when he was ready to hear it. When I get the timing right, he says something like 'Wow, I didn't think of it that way' and often changes his view."

The timing this COO is referring to here is when what is being said by a boss is in line with what he or she is expressing emotionally. To be sure that the alignment is sturdy, it's useful to listen for a while. Ask some questions. Dance around the topic somewhat before diving into it. You might say, "I've had some thoughts about our discussion. Would you like me to share them with you?" It's not likely that a boss will reply, "No, keep them to yourself!" And if the boss invites comments, he or she is partially responsible for hearing them. If you just launch into them without this preface, it's your neck that's at risk.

Interpreting on Two Levels

Another level of meaning you should listen for when reading between the lines is the connotation of the words used rather than just their denotation. Words have dictionary meanings, which are denotations, and common usage or implied meanings, which are connotations. If you listen only for denotations and fail to detect the implied meanings of a word or phrase, much of the meaning is lost. For example, if a letter of recommendation reads, "This candidate is promising and works hard. He deserves a chance," he's not likely to be hired—at least not where *I* work. The words are positive, but not positive enough. "Deserves a chance" seems to connote that he might be worth a risk. It doesn't suggest that the candidate is brimming over with potential. "Promising" and "works hard" are positive descriptors but could imply that while the candidate might one day make something of himself, he hasn't done so yet. Given that recommendations are usually more strongly worded, the negative connotations are what the reader is likely to come away with in this case rather than the denotations of the candidate description.

"He certainly is determined" could be a compliment. But if said out of the appropriate context or with a tone of voice that makes it sound as if this is all one can say for the person, the compliment is not what will be heard. "She certainly speaks her mind" could be a compliment. It could also imply that she is too aggressive. Reading between the lines means hearing not only what was said but what was meant as well.

I've devised a procedure to use in reading between the lines which I call the PURRR procedure. It's a kind of mind exercise routine to expand powers of observation:

The PURRR Procedure for Checking Assumptions

- PAUSE the next time you're about to formulate a judgment about a person based on something he or she has said or done.
- Make sure you UNDERSTAND (on content and relational levels) what the person meant by his or her words or actions, especially if "tact" seems to be operating.
- REFLECT briefly on the information you're using to form this judgment. Are there disconnects? If so, ask for more

information. Try asking some questions of the person (e.g., "Why do you think that?" or "Did you mean to say X?")

- REINTERPRET what just happened by applying an alternate favorable explanation to the one that you first considered.
- REDIRECT the conversation onto a path that best serves your goals.

Conveniently, this PURRR acronym suggests an image of a cat. And like a cat about to exit its pet door in the morning, the person following the PURRR procedure doesn't just dart outside before checking the terrain. If you've owned a cat or have observed cats, you know they don't take their surroundings for granted. They pause and reflect before entering new and even relatively familiar territory. This is one of those commonsense procedures not commonly applied by humans.

Let's suppose your usually easygoing boss is in a foul mood. He approaches you and angrily says, "I need that report tomorrow. No excuses." You weren't going to be late with the report. In fact, you never are. You are at a *choice point*. Do you get defensive? That depends on whether you've formulated an impression of him that begs a reaction rather than a response. You could say, "What's gotten into you today?" or "How'd I get in the line of fire?" But both of these call greater attention to the negative emotional component of the interaction. If you pause and realize that this is out of character, that he may be under a lot of pressure and that you just happen to be in the wrong place, other options become available. You might say, "I'll have it on your desk first thing in the morning." This response bypasses the relational (angry at you) component and focuses instead on the content of what he said (timely delivery of the report). It also does not engage him in an angry conflict at a point in time when he is acting out of character.

Suspending judgment and questioning inferences afford "wiggle room" in conversation. It's especially useful when dealing with people who are overbearing. As Ann Lewis observes, "There are a number of dinosaurs thrashing around and their tails can do some harm, but their brains are very small." She doesn't let herself slip into the trap of getting into a long conversation with the loudest person. With him or her as with everyone else, it's best to pause, understand, reflect, reinterpret, and redirect.

Using Finesse

To finesse a situation means to alter the perceptions of others in such subtle ways that most people fail to notice what you are doing. "Finesseurs" redefine events and manage perceptions to their advantage. Finesseurs do not believe a rose by any other name is still a rose. They place considerable stock in the power of words and actions. For them an impasse in negotiation can also be defined as an expected, momentary delay or the natural outcome of jet lag and long hours. If the latter reason is accepted, the course of action that logically follows is not angry termination of the negotiation, but rest and relaxation before reconvening in the light of a new day.

The artful politician not only knows how but also *when* to finesse. There's a timing element to casting advantageous perspectives on things. There is also an element of degree. When all the participants are deeply chagrined about losing an important contract, they certainly don't need "Jolly Jack" to bounce into the room and tell them that everything is just fine.

An artful *finesseur* who finds himself in a situation that his boss might see as negative looks for the wiggle room—the amount of perceptual space between reality and where he finds himself—and moves his boss through that space toward an advantageous vantage point for both the boss and himself. Sometimes all this takes is the clever alteration of word choice. The finesseur knows that often the only difference between a "problem" and an "opportunity" is a little redefinition.

We're finessed all the time at work and outside of it. Why do we pay more for a soda at a restaurant with luxurious ambience and formally attired waiters? Is the food that much better? Is the soda any different from that served at a nearby diner? No, we pay more because we've been finessed into believing that a soda should cost more in an elegant environment.

If we were honest, we'd even admit that being finessed can be very appealing. Eating at diners all the time could get tedious. Working in barren, colorless offices is hardly enjoyable. Being presented a gift that is not wrapped, or that has clearly been wrapped in haste, lessens the impact. When time and effort are put into a gift, the recipient is usually more impressed, even if the gift itself is something she was expecting.

To become somewhat more of a finesseur, you need to look at how you tend to define things happening to you and those around you. Look, too, at how well you package the information you're delivering. If you have a report due, why not make it look snazzy? Next time you give a presentation, break away from whatever is the norm and do something snappy. When you find yourself at a meeting where everyone is sinking into despair, find the silver lining.

This works well at work and in personal life too. My niece called me to tell me she'd become engaged. Of course, the topic of what our family now calls "the ring" came up. She described how her fiancé had given her a beautifully wrapped box containing a necklace. Upon removing the box, she found another elegant jewelry box that she thought might contain matching earrings. Instead, she opened the box to find a gorgeous diamond ring that, I later learned, the groom-to-be had spent considerable time selecting. Why didn't he just hand her the ring? Because there are times, perhaps more often than we realize, when finesse is a beautiful thing.

Effective finesseurs tend to see the glass as half full rather than half empty. They see opportunities where others see obstacles, problems become challenges, failures convert to learning experiences, delays become chances to catch their breath, and hard work turns into fun. Sometimes it's nice to have them around.

7.

The Art of Conversational Politics

———————■———————

Relationships emerge from interactions between people. We bring to each interaction sets of rules that tell us how we should act. For example, a subordinate may pause at a senior manager's office door awaiting an invitation because that is what he or she has learned is expected. The manager has the prerogative to welcome the subordinate or deny immediate access through verbal direction, such as "Please come back later," or by a nonverbal signal, such as a hand wave or a frown.

All communication is affected by implicit rules regarding who can say what to whom, as well as where, when, and how. People who reach the inner circle are the ones who've learned to identify and use these rules to their advantage. They've been students of conversational habits. They know that every comment has both a content and a relational meaning.[1] They also realize that they can process information centrally or peripherally.[2] Processing information centrally means that the person pays careful attention to it and treats it as relatively important. If, however, he or she is not interested in some information or for some reason does not see it as relevant to the issues at hand, it is likely to be processed peripherally. Little attention is given to information processed in this way.

The politically adept process information very selectively. They don't allow information to be processed peripherally until they determine its potential significance. They process it based on how it contributes to the goals they're attempting to achieve. Assume, for example, that you receive an abrupt memo from a superior. You could quickly dismiss the relevance of its abruptness or just as quickly reason that he or she was irritable when it was written, that if you're upset you're overreacting, or that memos have never been his or her strong suit, so you'd be overreacting if you were to give it any notice. The politically adept aren't so hasty. They may not dwell on the abruptness, but they won't dismiss it without determining whether it is an important part of the message.

Cues that provide information extras are rarely missed by the more politically savvy. You can't reach the inner circles of business by missing or misreading cues on a regular basis. It's important to become a sophisticated interpreter of meaning, observant of both content and relational levels of conversation, and careful in determining whether information is central or peripheral to your goals. This takes a considerable amount of mental effort at first, but in time it becomes second nature.

Start by doing some postmortems on critical conversations that seemed to have gone awry. While one is still fresh in your mind, consider what the content level was and whether the relational level altered that content in a way that you should have noticed. Consider, too, whether you should have processed some bits of information as more <u>central</u> or more <u>peripheral</u> than you did. Then consider how you might have acquired more information to be able to determine whether or not those cues were critical to an accurate interpretation of what was said. Could you have stepped back from the conversation and asked a question or two to derive a more accurate interpretation of the other person's meaning?

This process is fundamental to the achievement of the secret handshake. People who have made it to the top distrust surface meanings, and look deeper for implication and innuendo. When it suits them to respond to the content and ignore relational cues, they do so. For example, if your boss is in a foul mood and his comments are laced with personal attacks, you might want to ignore the tendency to reply to the attacks and instead reply to the content of his request. If the personal attacks continue when his mood has improved, there may be a relational message that is important. In this case, you might say in private to your boss, "I detected a slight edge in some things you said yesterday and again today. Is there something we should discuss?" The word "edge" is better than "jabs" or "insults" because it isn't as accusatory. It leaves your boss room to define the "edge" as due to something unrelated to your relationship if he chooses to do so. More accusatory terms don't leave this kind of wiggle room.

If the boss responds to your question by saying, "No, everything is fine," listen past what's been said. Do the nonverbal cues support this? Is everything fine in fact, or is he declining to discuss the issue? Do you have a sense that he thinks he shouldn't have to tell you what he meant because it's your job to know? If so, talk with someone who knows your boss well. Make sure it's someone you can trust. Get some advice. Determine whether what you've experienced is happening to others as well. Is it possible that the boss is temporarily out of sorts and that it has nothing to do with you? In other words, are you treating information that should be peripheral as if it's central? How does your colleague recommend responding? Should you drop the subject or pursue it? These are very important questions. Those who address them effectively experience greater career success.

It's worth mentioning here that the person from whom you seek advice can occasionally serve two purposes. If he or she knows the boss on a more personal level—perhaps they play golf together— then it may be possible for the adviser to intercede on your behalf by casually discussing the situation with the boss. He or she might put in a good word for you or mention that you're concerned about the latest relational downturn and that you'd like to patch things up if possible. You need to choose the person carefully. It should be someone who will present your concerns in a positive manner. Let him or her be the one to suggest talking to the boss. You can't get truly effective assistance from someone who feels compelled to provide it.

The Art of Conversational Steering

Politically adept people recognize that they're at least 75 percent responsible for how others treat them because each comment they make influences the responses of those to whom they're speaking.[3] Political sophistication requires the ability to steer conversations in directions conducive to one's goals.

A first step in becoming adept at conversational steering is to study how each person's input affects the options chosen by others. Consider the following exchange:

> **MARK:** Well, well, well . . . Look at who's on time for a change.
>
> **ED:** *(apologetically)* I'm rarely late.
>
> **MARK:** Oh-ho! We're feeling defensive as well!
>
> **ED:** *(looking at the floor)* Not really.
>
> **MARK:** *(smirking)* Sorry, Ed—but it sure seems that way to me.

Mark clearly has the upper hand in this brief exchange. He's in control of the direction of the conversation, and he is steering it straight toward a negative outcome for Ed. However, as mentioned before, every conversation, long or short, contains choice points where control is defined. In the above conversation, Ed can choose to take back some control. But before he can do so, he needs to be aware of how he relinquished control to Mark. A good way to do this is to look at the conversation in terms of directionality. All conversations consist of one-up, one-down, and one-across moves.[4] By using arrows, we can show who is attempting to take control over the direction of the conversation and who is relinquishing it. *One-up* moves (↑) involve control taking, *one-down* moves (↓) involve control giving, and *one-across* moves (→) are essentially neutral.

> **MARK:** Well, well, well . . . Look at who's on time for a change. (↑)
>
> **ED:** *(apologetically)* I'm rarely late. (↓)
>
> **MARK:** Oh-ho! We're feeling defensive as well! (↑)
>
> **ED:** *(looking at the floor)* Not really. (↓)
>
> **MARK:** Sorry, Ed—but it sure seems that way to me. (↑)

Mark has assumed control because Ed has failed to act at each choice point to regain the control that Mark has claimed. When Mark makes the initial accusation of general lateness, Ed weakly defends himself. Mark uses that weakness to accuse Ed of defensiveness, which Ed somewhat sheepishly denies—once again giving Mark control of the situation.

Each time someone either says something to you or nonverbally conveys a message to you, a choice point occurs. If the conversation is of a type in which you've been engaged many times, you may enact it without ever thinking in terms of choice. If Ed, for example, is always defensive or if he is easily provoked to apologize, Mark will quickly learn that he can manage Ed into a negative outcome. Mark knows, consciously or not, that Ed will fail to take advantage of the choice points in the conversation. Instead of pondering whether Ed will *respond* in an unexpected manner, Mark can count on Ed to *react* predictably and, in this case, weakly.

Let's look again at the Mark and Ed scenario. Ed can change the direction of the conversation by making a one-up move or a one-across move at each *choice point*. Here's one possibility:

MARK: Well, well, well . . . Look at who's on time for a change. (↑)
ED: Whoa, Mark, that was a deadly cut. You must have been practicing that all night *(smiles)*. (↑)

Here Ed meets Mark's one-up move with a sarcastic one-up of his own. Maybe he'll get a laugh. Of course, if Mark is Ed's boss, he'll probably want to be less cutting in his retort. So he might respond like this:

MARK: Well, well, well . . . Look at who's on time for a change. (↑)
ED: *(smiling slightly)* Surf wasn't up today. (↑)

If Mark appreciates this kind of comeback, Ed will actually be better off than if he had become defensive. However, if Ed *is* chronically late, this may be too flippant a reply. He might want to say with the same slight smile:

ED: I've turned over a new leaf. (↑)

or

ED: I bought a new watch. (↑)

These comments inject mild humor, bypass insult, avoid defensiveness, and, more important, imply that he intends to be on time in the future.

If you often find yourself reacting to people in ways that are not advancing your chances of success, it's time to look at whether you should be making one-up comments instead of one-down ones, or vice versa. Also assess whether you tend to slip into one-ups or one-downs when you could buy yourself a little time with an occasional one-across comment, such as "I hadn't thought of it that way," "That's interesting," "Hmmm," or "I see what you mean." In other words, steer your conversations by intercepting your predictable reactions.

Developing a Repertoire of Responses

In my role as coach, I teach people to expand their repertoires of response options. Those who do so feel liberated because they're no longer stuck in dysfunctional scripts. They're in charge of where their conversations go.

At every point in conversation, we have a choice of focus. We can respond to what is said or to what is meant. When neither option is likely to lead to a positive outcome, a politically sophisticated player fabricates a desirable meaning and responds to that one. Humor often works this way. At a meeting, one of your peers says, "What you're saying makes no sense." You have some choices here. Do you respond to this one-up comment as a reasonable observation, an insult, or a challenge? The choice is yours. If you decide to treat it as a reasonable observation, your response might be, "I thought the same thing the first time this idea came to mind, but I'll tell you why I no longer see it that way." Should you decide to treat the comment as a minor insult, you could respond with humor: "Listen, Einstein, I'm not finished yet!" To be taken lightly, this response would benefit from the accompaniment of a slight smile signaling to the other person that you're playing. If you treat the comment as a challenge, you could say, "You're absolutely right. It doesn't make sense at first but it will shortly." Then you continue, being sure to clarify all points until the challenger and those around him or her appear satisfied.

As you can see, another critical part of conversational self-edification involves creating options for yourself so that you don't fall into conversational traps. Bill Foltz, senior executive with a high-tech venture-capital firm, is amazed at how predictable people allow themselves to become. "I told one of my guys that I'd love to play poker with him because I always know what he's thinking." Foltz considers this kind of self-imposed entrapment a sure way to fall off the road to the inner circle. "Being predictable is one of the worst things you can be in business." It makes you uninteresting, even tedious. Clearly, that is not a career enhancer.

The president of a European clothes manufacturer told me this story when we were talking about the disadvantages of predictability. The brother of a wealthy deceased man was attempting to wrest the estate away from the man's widow. He claimed that the deceased brother hadn't run the business and therefore was not entitled to bequeath half of it to his wife. The lawyer for the widow didn't know the complainant personally, but a niece in the family happened to tell the lawyer that the brother had a tendency to brag. Some time later, when the case came to trial, the brother took the witness stand.

"I hear you are a well-traveled man," the lawyer suggested. The brother agreed. "You've probably seen more of the world than any ten people in this room," the lawyer offered.

Agreeing once again, the proud man began to regale the attorney and everyone else in the courtroom with descriptions of his many journeys.

"How often would you say you travel?" the attorney asked.

"I'm on the road more than half the year," the man replied.

The attorney paused, and let this fact sink in with the court. "Tell me, then, who was it that took care of the family business while you were away on all these trips?"

The brother began to stutter and then went silent.

"Tell us who ran the business," the attorney insisted. "Surely with all your traveling it couldn't have been you."

"No, it was my brother," the plaintiff admitted, losing the case in that instant.

The attorney had led the proud brother into a trap. By learning just one predictable behavior—a tendency to brag—the attorney was able to win the case and save the widow's inheritance.

Predictability is a career kiss of death. Versatility is critical to reaching the upper levels of most businesses. So just when others expect you to argue over an issue that isn't critical, consider saying,

"This idea has promise" or "I now see where you're going with this plan." When they expect you'll be defensive, don't be. If they suspect you'll be a roadblock to progress, be a facilitator instead. Ask where you can be of assistance. And when it looks as if everyone thinks you'll be angry if your idea isn't adopted, interject with "I like this plan." Don't overdo this strategy. A little unpredictable behavior here, a little there, and soon you'll find doors open to you that had been previously closed when everyone knew exactly what you'd say and do.

Separating Offense from Insult

People easily offend and are offended by others. We may offend by being too abrupt or by indicating annoyance or exasperation with another person—even when it may not be the person but the subject at hand that is causing our annoyance or exasperation. All day every day, people accidentally offend each other. If you slip easily into an offensive posture each time someone accidentally offends you, life becomes like old Dodge City on a bad day.

Handling accidental offense requires versatility. A good sense of humor can come in handy. If someone doesn't return your phone call, you could chastise him or her in front of others. You could avoid eye contact. You could reciprocate in kind. But all of these are overkill responses to unintentional offense. If it really bothers you, try sending an e-mail instead of using the phone. Perhaps the offender responds more quickly to electronic mail than to voice mail.

An *insult* is a purposeful attempt to make someone feel or look bad—or both. One way to tell if you've been accidentally offended or purposefully insulted is to inform the person who upset you that you did not appreciate his remark. If he does it again, then you know you've been insulted, and that calls for a stronger response than accidental offense would merit. Remaining calm

An alternative technique to meeting insult with insult is to *give other people the opportunity to do the right thing.* If you present an idea at a meeting and someone disparages its value, you might say, "Let's not be hasty. Bear with me a bit longer while I explain how this will benefit us." (↑) Suppose your detractor, rather than doing the right thing, tries again to interrupt you by saying, "This is a waste of time." (↑) At this point, you have indeed been insulted and everybody knows it. What should you do? Sure, you could say, "Your attitude is creating the real waste of time." (↑) It's usually better, though, to take and hold the higher ground. One option is to say, "Perhaps you're right, and then again perhaps not. [Look away from the detractor and toward the others in the room.] I'll take just a few more moments to describe an alternate view and then we can all decide." (↑)

All of these options are aimed at denying your detractor the upper hand by making you less predictable. By remaining calm and showing judgment and maturity despite good reason to do otherwise, you essentially one-up the offender in an unexpected way. This is the "business meeting" equivalent of the karate black belt ignoring the barroom insults of a drunken bully. You acknowledge your detractor's concern, you respond in a manner that gives you the floor, and then you promise anyone who believes that the detractor could be right that you won't take much time demonstrating that he or she isn't. Who wins? You do, by showing grace under fire. People remember that.

Suppose a problem develops in your area and someone charges, "You are to blame for this situation." This is an insult. Should you counterattack? It depends on the stakes. Usually, it's better to explore the conditions before launching a counterattack. Here are some responses that buy time to develop a cogent response:

A. "The real issue is how to correct the problem." (↑)
B. "Interesting that you see it that way." (→)
C. "I'm not convinced that blame is the primary issue." (↑)

If said calmly, response A keeps you from slipping into a defensive reaction. If it's followed by "Let's see how we can rectify this situation," it displays a refusal to engage in relational attack and instead focuses on concern for the issue at hand.

Response B is a one-across move; it neither admits nor denies blame, and it neither takes control nor gives it away. It avoids being pulled into defensiveness but refuses to give credence to the attack. This response demonstrates the utility of one-across moves.

Response C redirects the attack, and, if followed by an expression of interest in finding a way to rectify the situation, it can focus both parties on constructive action.

To become and remain effective in day-to-day conversational politics, this ability to redirect conversations is crucial. The politically adept are rarely pulled into dysfunctional conversation patterns (DCPs).[5] They manage conversations the way an expert chess player manages the moves and gambits of the game.

Handling Politically Pivotal Moments

Managing conversations becomes particularly difficult when emotions take over. Usually, this happens when what researchers call "tactics of social diminution" are applied. Among them are placing blame, ridiculing, eliciting guilt, alienating, dismissing, steamrollering, humiliating, denouncing, and scapegoating.[6] If you can see such traps being laid for you, you are much more likely to be able to divert, dodge, redirect, or otherwise avoid them. This is important. How you handle yourself when confronted with these kinds of career pivotal situations indicates to others whether or not you're becoming a "player." And people are less likely to "mess" with a player.

I remember an incident that took place at a professional conference when I was a young researcher. It was the first time I had ever sat on a panel of esteemed colleagues, all of whom had far more experience and visibility as scholars than I did. Before an audience of hundreds of communication researchers, one of these barely gray eminences, a man who was well known for his caustic attacks on others in his field, stepped to the podium and began objecting to my presence on the panel. Rather than tell us about his work, he denounced *my* work. He complained bitterly that I was far too young to have made the kind of research contribution that would entitle me to sit with such an august panel of experts (in which category he included himself of course).

In all honesty, I, too, had been wondering why I was on the panel. I *was* young, but then again, I told myself, I'd written a well-regarded book. Yet here was a self-proclaimed expert publicly and pompously pronouncing my inadequacy. As I looked out at the audience, I saw that all five hundred or so persons were watching me, some with evident sympathy, others in empathic trauma. Most of what this man was saying about my recent book had no basis in fact. It didn't even sound remotely familiar. Some ten minutes of the twenty minutes allocated for this professor to speak had already passed, and he was still berating me. I thought it would never end. Then I noticed a friend of mine sitting well away from me in the middle of the large hall. She was watching me intently. When she saw that she had my eye, she raised her left hand and silently slammed her right fist into it. The signal was clear: Give this guy all you've got.

Finally, it was my turn to speak. As I stood up and walked slowly to the podium, I could feel the eyes of everyone in the audience follow me. I methodically unfolded my notes and allowed my eyes to traverse the room, looking at the people assembled to witness my career's early demise. This was, I sensed, a pivotal moment. In as calm a voice as I could manage, I began: "I could spend my whole twenty minutes with you today responding to my colleague, but that would be a decided waste of our time. Let me start my presentation by quoting him, an indication that at least I've actually *read* his work."

The audience howled with laughter and broke into applause. Here was a young woman who should have died a thousand deaths from such humiliation. Instead I had humorously dismissed the critic and, to my delight, it worked. When the session ended, the other panelists were still smiling as they approached me. They expressed their annoyance with the offending professor and their pleasure at seeing me stand up to him. The most esteemed of them, Gerald Miller, told me, "You're going to be okay. They now know to watch out for you."

It was a good lesson for me, and I'll be forever grateful to my friend who, by directing me to break out of the demure script my enemy was attempting to create for me, helped me to move from embarrassment to calculated anger to effective action. Of course, had my detractor's attack not been so "over the top," his comments would have warranted a more reasoned rebuttal. Had it been reasonably delivered, I would have been obliged to respond more extensively to his criticisms.

The attack on me was decidedly relational and self-serving, rather than a cogent, constructive critique. Therefore, the response had to be relational, yet one that did not validate his slurs with a bitter counterattack.

I've not always been so fortunate as to be able to think of what to say in such situations. Another day, another situation, and the young person I was might have been pulled into a dysfunctional script. It was my first lesson in what I've learned is a key political axiom: *You can't play in the big leagues if you let them look good at your expense.* The easiest way to get snookered into such a position is to react rather than respond. Don't allow yourself to be pulled into an attack, as a spider pulls prey into its web.

People still come up to me at academic conferences to say they remember the day I put the barely gray eminence in his place. "I don't think I could have done it," many of them have said. But then again, it's hard to say what you'll do when so much depends on the decision. Because that event was so public, if I'd responded in a demure, apologetic way, that, too, would have been remembered. And who needs that kind of track record?

The Beauty of a Well-Placed Question

It's easy enough for me to advise you to avoid engaging in dysfunctional communication patterns, where what you say and do can be predicted by the people who know you. It's another thing to actually change this behavior. By their very nature, conversational patterns are ingrained habits. Like getting into our cars in the morning, we can slip into them and turn on the engine without even noticing. Unlike our cars, however, DCPs take us where we don't want to go: into unfortunate communication outcomes.

So the next time you can't think of a quick, effective response, buy yourself some time. One technique for doing this is to ask a well-placed question. Unless we ask questions, we are forced to operate on our assumptions, which is an easy way to fall into a DCP. Questions can have the marvelous side effect of directing conversations away from DCPs.

Businesspeople find it difficult to ask questions, particularly in Western cultures. Questions seem to have gotten a bad rap. One reason is the feared potential side effect of losing face. No one wants to appear as if he or she doesn't know what is going on, even if that is the reality. Questions may suggest ignorance, or that the questioner has not prepared or listened well. Asking a question may be seen as a one-down move, inviting an unwelcome lecture or advice.

An otherwise very effective sales manager for one of the largest temporary placement services in Southern California was having considerable difficulty with one of his people. She contradicted him constantly. When he and I talked, he was about to fire her. His hesitation to do so came from her excellent sales record. She was largely responsible for his division's success. He assumed that her strong record made her feel comfortable with publicly contradicting him.

What this manager had not considered is the contribution he was making to the dysfunctional pattern. He'd allowed a DCP to develop. When she interrupted, corrected, or overrode his ideas with her own, he rolled his eyes and glared at her but said nothing. He never asked her why she was responding to him in such unorthodox ways. I suggested he invite her to lunch to ask her about the annoying habits. "Hear her out," I advised. "Assess whether she is aware of your annoyance." We planned how he'd respond.

He telephoned me the next week. "I can't believe it," he said. "She's a different person. She told me at lunch that she was wondering why I kept shooting her glances and looking perturbed when she was just trying to help. I explained that her idea of helping was not mine. It seemed as if she was attempting to take control. We came up with some ways for her to communicate more effectively with me. We cleared the air, and ever since then she's been making her suggestions in ways that are productive."

It takes practice to use questions in a manner that avoids unnecessary altercations. Here's a practice scenario. Consider how you'd use questions to reverse the negativity in the following situation.

Let's say that Steve, a VP of international sales, is having difficulty with an up-and-coming middle manager, Matt, who has recently been transferred to his division. Steve's company is becoming increasingly global. Matt's arrival has antagonized many people because many of his interactions with subsidiary managers in other countries have resulted in verbal altercations. Steve would like to reassign Matt, but Steve's boss, Paul, executive VP of sales and marketing, prides himself on having a good eye for talent and he sees Matt as a rising star. This is how a conversation between Steve and Paul might proceed:

STEVE: Matt is upsetting all our producers in France, Germany, and Japan. He's clueless when it comes to working with people in other cultures. (↑)
PAUL: He has a good head on his shoulders. Just give him time and he'll adapt. (↑)

STEVE: I can't afford that kind of time, Paul. Three months can ruin a lot of relationships. (↑)

PAUL: Maybe you're just not mentoring him adequately. (↑)

STEVE: I spend half my time with him. (↑)

PAUL: I don't want him failing on your watch. (↑)

STEVE: He should be reassigned before the damage is irreversible. (↑)

PAUL: He stays and that's final. Find a way to make it work. (↑)

These kinds of interactions occur daily all over the world. Steve and Paul have tossed the "hot potato" back and forth, but at no time did they acknowledge that they're on the same team. The conversation focused on differences of opinion and ended with an unemphatic, misguided solution. Neither person asked any questions. No one made a one-across or one-down move. Each of them presented his interests but failed to explore connections and mutually beneficial outcomes. Before reading on, consider where Steve or Paul might have altered the course of this conversation with a question.

Since Steve reports to Paul, it's to his advantage to connect rather than spar over Matt's future. Paul also has a lot to gain from finding a reasonable solution. If Paul took the lead in redirecting the conversation onto a more productive course, it might go more like this:

STEVE: Matt is upsetting all his producers in France, Germany, and Japan. He's clueless when it comes to working with people in other cultures. (↑)

PAUL: He has a good head on his shoulders. Just give him time and he'll adapt. (↑)

STEVE: I can't afford that kind of time, Paul. Three months can ruin a lot of relationships. (↑)

PAUL: What are our options here? (↓)

STEVE: Transferring him out is the best one. (↑)

PAUL: Probably so from the vantage point of a quick fix, but not in terms of developing him. I think he has a contribution to make. (↑) Got any other ideas?(↓)

STEVE: The problem right now is to get him away from the phone. (↑) What if we send him to Europe, have him tag along with one of the guys he actually gets along with? (↓) We could have him undergo intense cultural training before he leaves. That way, we'd put some time between him and the people he's offended—it would give me time to mend some fences. (↑)

PAUL: It's worth thinking about. (→)

In this conversation, Paul has connected with Steve. He hasn't reacted to Steve's remark that he couldn't afford three more months of Matt. Instead, Paul has posed a question: "What are our options here?" This has taken the conversation down a less defensive track. Steve has responded by suggesting, not demanding, a transfer for Matt. This time, Paul didn't react with an emphatic "Can't do it." He empathized with Steve's interests, but sought more thinking. Once both began probing for a solution rather than placing blame and dueling, they were on their way toward a workable solution.

Because of their face-losing potential, it's useful to learn how to ask questions in ways that don't imply ignorance on your part. "What are our options here?" if asked by Paul in a tone and manner that invites ideas—rather than one that suggests he has absolutely no good thoughts of his own—allows the question to break the DCP while not sacrificing Paul's credibility. "Have we explored all the alternatives?" and "Is there a chance that we're moving too quickly here?" are two additional options. It's important to have questions like these in your response repertoire.

What If the Pressure Is On?

What really separates the artful political player from the novice is conversational agility under pressure. Here again the key is to respond rather than react, employ strategically one-up, one-down, and one-across moves. Steven Sample, president of the University of Southern California, says the first mistake people make in pressure situations is to assume that they always need to "go in looking powerful." Sample told me how one of his mentors, Sam Regenstrief, did just the opposite. Sam was president of a leading appliance manufacturing company. "He had poor eyesight, Coke-bottle glasses, and a kind of dyslexia when it came to talking. So he sometimes appeared to be a dumb country bumpkin. That led everyone with whom we negotiated to think they had us over a barrel. Sam asked them to repeat things, seemed to mix things, up, and often appeared befuddled. Frustrated by this time-consuming roundabout route to consensus, the other side almost always revised the deal to our liking. Sam would walk away with the better part of the deal every time." Sample told me that Sam's power wasn't in a stand-tall, rush-the-enemy approach, but in his ability to disarm people with his unexpected, slow, vulnerable, "easy pickin's" style.

I asked Sample whether that same style works for him. "No, not for university presidents," he said. "You just can't be a bumpkin. But I learned a lot from Sam." When the pressure is on, Sample recommends that you listen and hold back, take what people say in bits, go off on some tangents at times and then circle back to the main topic from a different direction. Sample also knows there are some things he won't say. "I never say, 'No, absolutely not' or 'This isn't negotiable.' I keep flexible, ask people to tell me more, and stay on the lookout for a new, better direction."

Sample told me that while most of us might prefer to deny it, "As you move closer to the top, people skills dominate over technical skills." No one wants to think the Nobel Prize is given to the best talker, and in actual fact it isn't. But as Sample says of many top prizes and honors, including the secret handshake, "You have to have made a stellar contribution to get into the holding tank to be seriously considered at all. But after that, it's politics. You need to be known and respected by former winners, people on the selection committees and people who know them. You generally can't rank order people at the highest level on the basis of their technical achievements, so it's relationships that often make the final difference."

What this means is that no matter how high up you go, no matter how much pressure to achieve you've put behind you, if you want the top brass ring, you need to handle people delicately. Producer/director Deborah Hill has taught herself to do this. She describes herself as "direct." And her days are full of pressure. Yet, she also says, "I pick my battles, share the power, never say no, learn how they think and let some of my ideas appear to be theirs." Like Sample, she believes relationships are crucial to getting things done. She keeps options open and strives to find workable solutions.

While working on the movie *The Fisher King* with Terry Gilliam of Monty Python fame, Hill made a difficult situation work. "Terry wanted an interior tower to match an exterior one for one of the scenes. I looked into it. The cost was just too high. I reluctantly told Terry that we couldn't justify paying $100,000 to have a tower in a walk-through scene. He was disappointed. I could have said, 'It can't be done,' but instead I thought about how Terry thinks. He's intrigued by special effects. So I surprised him by offering a hanging foreground miniature. After some research, it became clear that we could make a tower four feet high and have the camera shoot from below. Terry loved the idea. He still got his tower, we used a novel special effects approach, which he loved, and it only cost us $17,000. Everyone was happy."

The next time you're about to shut down a discussion with someone whose relationship you value because something she wants can't be done or doesn't seem practical, back away from the decision point. Consider what matters to her. What does she really need? It might not be as difficult to provide as you think. Hill told me about a "needy writer" who insisted on seeing her immediately on one of her busiest days. "I told the president of my company, that there was no need to see this writer. She said, 'Listen, he just needs you to hold his hand a little. That's all he really wants.' " Hill's resentment dissolved with that explanation. "I realized that she was right. He wasn't asking for a lot. He just needed my reassurance and a little of my time. So that's what I gave him."

The politically adept know that often a good deal of circling around the real issue goes on in conversation. They listen past the circles for what truly matters to the person. Often they find it takes very little to provide a satisfactory response, thus saving one more relationship from premature demise.

What If They Kill the Messenger?

Lieutenant General Claudia Kennedy believes in letting her superiors know about her significant concerns, pressing for change but then leaving it to them to get it done. In every organization there's a limited amount of telling people above you that they've made mistakes and winning at their expense before it hurts your career. If people were keen on getting bad news, why would they so frequently "kill the messenger"? When it's about their own inadequacies, they're especially testy. The truth is that we all have inadequacies. It's better, therefore, to deliver potentially offensive information in ways that lessen the offensive quality.

"I always pose my arguments in terms of what the army needs," General Kennedy told me. "That's where I focus—not on the person's error, but on what it's doing to the one thing we all care deeply about." This approach depersonalizes what might be received as a threat. Focus away from the person and on your mutual goal. Kennedy told me of a time when she felt compelled to inform her superiors of the prevalence of offensive materials posted around a barracks. "They didn't like hearing about it," she told me. "But it was too important to let it pass." She described to me how she purposely stayed away from placing blame, focused on the problem, explained why it was harmful to the army, disputed the veracity of some proffered excuses that would have dismissed the issue, and then let them handle it. Kennedy believes that in the majority of cases, if your reasoning is sufficiently solid, those above you will take it upon themselves to make the change either this time or next time around. If you don't want to be one of the killed messengers, make your point, make it well, and get on with things.

Among the most politically adept conversational skills is the ability to let bygones be bygones. Deborah Hill considers one of the paramount political skills the ability to "lose gracefully." Nearly every secret handshake holder I interviewed for this book mentioned this conversational skill as crucial to getting ahead. You've got to put things behind you. We all have bad experiences. The secret to success is the ability to move on. This doesn't mean you aren't entitled to a few hours or days of sputtering, but, with few exceptions, when the dust clears it's time to get on with things. Pounding people into submission or reminding them over and over of their past errors doesn't do anything except get a lot of people very angry. And you can be sure that they'll pay you back in kind someday.

The Political Dance

If you've already gone too far with your criticism of someone or if you've attempted to pound him or her into submission, there are subtle ways of "making up." One common one I call the political dance. It involves complimenting someone who expects you to attack him because the two of you are at odds. If he follows your lead, he'll compliment you. Perhaps you've observed people who were hurling insults at a prior meeting saying things like "I like the idea Bill just proposed." Within minutes, not to be outdone, Bill reciprocates with a positive comment about some idea advanced by the person who just complimented him. And the dance goes on. Sometimes it's a waltz with positive regard surreptitiously slipped in. Sometimes it's a rumba with compliments flowing and intimacy visibly present. One person makes the lead compliment, another follows, and then the roles reverse.

In the best dancing, it isn't clear who is leading. There's no heavy-handed pushing and shoving. Similarly, in political dancing, it's important to avoid the appearance of contrived, self-serving compliments. They must make sense in the context of what you're saying. They should appear natural, not forced. "Jack's insight was critical to the progress we've made on X" is an example of linking the compliment to the context of what is being discussed. Greater subtlety can be achieved by placing the person's name deeper in the comment instead of up front. "The progress we've made to date is impressive, thanks in large part to Jack's early insights." When this kind of conversational dancing is done well, it's a beautiful thing. It demonstrates that you've moved on, put harm behind you, forgotten slights and gratuitous attacks. This garners respect and moves you closer to the inner circle.

In Review

Conversations are the building blocks of careers. As such they make access to the inner circle possible or deprive people of it. Some of the conversational enhancements you can apply immediately are these:

- Attend to both content and relational meanings in conversation. Look for cues indicating that what was said may not be what was meant. Consider whether information is central or peripheral before acting upon it.

- Respond to a different interpretation than the one intended if that one is leading down a problematic path. Be creative.

- Conduct some postmortems on a few conversations that didn't work for you. Where did you misread cues? Could you have ignored a cue that took you away from your goal?

• Observe people who are expert at redirecting conversations away from danger points. Experiment with their techniques.

• Engage allies in the interpretation process. Find someone trustworthy who can read meanings well, ones who can offer advice on how to help you avoid relational downturns with key people.

• Learn to recognize choice points in conversations, places where you might slip into dysfunctional scripts. Practice versatility in one-up, one-down, and one-across moves. Avoid predictability.

• Separate offense from insult. Don't treat them the same. Whenever possible, give an offender the opportunity to do the right thing.

• Acquire some clever retorts to put-downs.

• When a response isn't on the tip of your tongue, buy yourself some time with a question or two.

• When the pressure is on, respond rather than react. Don't get backed into a corner or back others into one. Stay flexible, be on the lookout for mutual gain options, and when necessary step away to discuss the topic at another time.

• Don't frequently bring up bad news or remind people of their foibles. Lace criticism with compliment. Position issues in terms of mutual concern.

- Don't be too quick to say no. Listen for what really matters to people. You may be able to deliver with less effort than you think.

- Move on after an altercation. Let go. Show them that you don't carry a grudge even if you're still a little hot under the collar.

- Practice political dancing. Be subtle in your lead, natural in the positioning of your compliments.

8.

When Politics Gets Heavy-Handed

———■———

In companies where politics is rampant, the games can get rough, even overtly so. "Hatchet men" do the dirty work so their bosses can "keep their hands clean." When people see such behaviors rewarded, they often become commonplace.

When incivility rules, it is often the result of a tit-for-tat mentality. Instigators see their actions as legitimate or moralistic because they are providing "just deserts" for those who have offended them. In this way, dysfunctional communication patterns can quickly become the norm. In cases where incivility occurs between senior managers and those who work for them, the result can be a decline in productivity. Subordinates collude to resist authority, and purposeful errors, destructive conflict, absenteeism, and rumors escalate.

The result of this tit-for-tat behavior is a spiral of incivility. When such spirals are unchecked, the incivility ultimately spreads throughout the entire organization, much like a virus for which there is no antidote.

The best way to prevent spirals of incivility is to address acts of rudeness and injustice swiftly and with justice. To do so, you need to be able to identify them, especially the more subtle, insidious forms. This chapter is devoted to defining a number of negative games that might exist in your organization, along with strategies for defusing them.

Damning with Faint Praise

This political maneuver is used when people don't want to be perceived as saying or writing something negative about a target person. Instead, they praise the person in a pointedly halfhearted manner. This letter of recommendation is an example: "Mary has worked with me for ten years. She is a good person who can be relied upon to do as asked. I've always admired her humor. Many people like her. She is on time every day and takes only those days allotted to her each year. She enjoys teamwork and has come up with some good ideas. I like Mary."

The letter isn't worth the paper it's written on unless the person writing it is trying to kill Mary's chances of getting promoted or getting another job. While there's nothing overtly negative in this letter, it doesn't contain the kind of hyperbole expected in letters of recommendation. The reader is inclined to believe that the writer's real message is: "Mary doesn't have much going for her."

This same effect can be obtained verbally. Public praise can shape perceptions in ways that help some people get ahead and cause others to languish. "Mike should be congratulated for his outstanding work on this project. Stand up, Mike, and take a bow. Your ideas have saved us a considerable amount of money. We're also grateful to Mike's teammate, Bill. Thanks, Bill." In contrast to the praise heaped on Mike, Bill receives a passing mention with nothing specific about his contribution. People are left to assume that either Bill accomplished significantly less than Mike or he's out of favor. If you happen to be Bill, you might feel that you'd have been better served if your contribution had been completely overlooked.

It's difficult to deal with faint praise because it's so deniable. If Bill stands and says sarcastically, "Thanks for the wildly enthusiastic praise," he risks looking like a selfish fool. Of course, if he lets such faint praise pass without comment, then various uncomplimentary assumptions may be made about him. Some may think he is out of favor with senior management, and so they'll avoid him to prevent being associated with an out-group member. Others may pity him, but that's at least as unsavory an outcome. And Bill's boss is likely to repeat this damning by faint praise unless Bill speaks up in some fashion.

In such circumstances, a fair amount of reading between the lines is required to determine the best response. If Bill believes he's on the way out and his boss is just helping that process along, then he has nothing to lose by standing up for himself. If he has misread the situation, though, and accuses the boss of purposely undervaluing him when the boss in fact was trying to give Mike a well-deserved ego boost, Bill may antagonize his boss.

The best response in a given situation depends to some extent on the nature of the relationship and the culture of the organization. If Bill has a good relationship with his boss and the culture of the company or division is one of open discussion, he might later in the day say to his boss, "Mike seemed to have gotten the lion's share of the credit today." If it works well, the boss will explain why he gave Mike so much more credit. Bill may discover that his boss didn't realize that he'd done so. Bill would then know that he'd been offended rather than insulted. And as mentioned in chapter 7, the accidental nature of offense calls for a more understanding response than that called for by intended insult.

Having let his boss know of his concern, Bill has at least achieved an important step. If the boss has good intentions, he will be more likely to publicly praise Bill next time the opportunity arises. This approach is better than letting rage fester. The outcome of rage suppression is rarely positive.

Before making choices in situations like this, it's important to know what it is you want to get out of it. Does Bill want an apology? Does he want recognition at the next meeting? Does he simply want to be sure that his boss knows how much he contributed? Often people try rectifying a bad situation before considering the solution they're after. If Bill cares less about public recognition than he cares about his boss's opinion of him, then he might say, "I'm not concerned about what others think, but I want to be sure you're pleased with my work." The solution he is looking for should inform the tactics he chooses.

Public Put-Downs

Overt insults and put-downs are other ways people may try to achieve a momentary advantage, or leave a lasting scar. Among the common put-downs are direct insults, interruptions, caustic criticism, disregard, patronizing comments, exclusion from a conversation, blocking conversational input, lying in wait, and tripping up.

Some of these tactics are used face-to-face and some are used behind the scenes.

I was recently treated to one of those character-building experiences that test one's communication reflexes. The University of Southern California was honoring Warren Bennis for his major contribution to the study of leadership with a daylong conference attended by leading business scholars and practitioners.[1] It was a marvelous, star-studded event. The audience was as august as the panel members.

I'd spent every spare moment of the week prior to the conference pondering how my remarks opening the second afternoon panel might provide provocative thought while also honoring Warren. I developed a short tribute showing how Warren's uncanny ability to predict future business possibilities was balanced by his passion for knowledge from the past. "There is no intellectual well," I said to the two-hundred-plus audience of leading lights, "from which Warren has not drunk."

I then introduced the panel of impressive speakers: Tom Stewart, member of the board of editors of *Fortune* magazine; Jeffrey Sonnenfeld, author of five books and chairman and president of the Chief Executive Leadership Institute; Mihaly Czikszentmihalyi, professor and author famous for introducing the concept of flow[2]; and Tom Peters, author of *The Pursuit of Excellence* and self-described "prince of disorder, champion of bold failures, and maestro of zest."

It was my not-so-enviable task to hold each of these panelists to a fifteen-minute presentation. Tom Stewart presented first. His was an eloquent description of trust made even more impressive by his having conveyed it within his fifteen allotted minutes.

As Stewart returned to his chair, Tom Peters strode to the front of the room. He proceeded to speak at his characteristic frenetic pace, loudly tossing his thoughts to the assembled masters. I knew immediately that he would not look over at me to determine his remaining time. There were two speakers behind Peters, each deserving their fifteen minutes. It was my job to assure that they would have it. At approximately the fifteen-minute point, I noticed Tom Stewart looking at his watch. He'd stayed within his limit and was probably wondering if Peters would be expected to stay within his. I wrote "1 minute" in large print on my yellow-lined pad and attempted to hold it where Peters might catch a glimpse. It was no use. Pressing toward seventeen minutes, I put a line through the "1 minute" and was about to hold up the pad when Peters suddenly halted. He was standing with his back to me and the other panelists and was looking directly at Warren, seated in the front row.

In a million years I could not have predicted what would happen next. "What is this stuff about balance we just heard?" Peters scoffed, arms flailing, not mentioning my name, not even glancing in my direction. "Isn't that just about the worst compliment you've ever . . . ?" I hardly heard the last word. The audience hushed, Warren looked at me, and what must have been a nanosecond seemed an eternity. Here was one of the most famous management writers of our time telling my friend and esteemed colleague that I'd just given him perhaps the worse insult of his life.

The final word of Peters's attack had not even finished rolling off his tongue when, with heart pounding, my body raised abruptly from the chair. Pointing at Peters, I said emphatically with the slight smile of a sparring partner up to the task, "Your time . . . is up!" The audience roared with delight. Peters turned to look at me. He paused, then smiled. Stewart nudged my arm as I slowly sat down, all the time pointing Peters to his chair. "That was priceless," Stewart whispered, "just priceless."

The audience was still chortling when Peters attempted to regain his stride. He walked to the center of the room and took a deep breath indicative of a topic change and likely a fresh beginning to many more overtime minutes, when I said pleasantly but firmly, "Your time really is up, Tom." Peters looked from me to the audience, now once again in ripples of laughter, dropped his notes to his side, and to his credit, said with a smile, "I guess my time is up." They laughed again.

After the panel Peters explained that he knew that I hadn't described Warren in the way he'd represented it. He said, "You know how it is. We speakers use each other. And that's what I did to you." I paused and chose to respond to the spirit of his remarks, the relational level. This wasn't the time for a lengthy debate about the virtues and vices of using people. The post-panel press of people taking photos was increasing by the second. I merely said, smiling but with direct eye contact, "And I fixed you for that, Tom." He returned the smile and replied in a manner acknowledging a good battle, "Yes, you did."

Throughout the rest of the conference and during dinner that evening, one person after another congratulated me on quick thinking and graceful, witty retort. Many said they couldn't have said what I'd said, not that quickly and especially not to Tom Peters. But Peters had twisted words I'd crafted carefully to honor someone for whom I had high regard. Was there a choice? I might have let Peters twist my words. I might have gotten angry and stormed out of the room. I could have said, "Get your own material!," which might have been quite funny. I might have done a host of things. But, first and foremost, he was a guest. My role as panel moderator gave me an opportunity to humorously but emphatically shut down an attack, and I took it. When put-downs exceed your threshold, when they threaten your standing among those you respect, action is better than inaction.

Madeline Larson, whom we met in chapter 4, minimizes the likelihood of public personal attacks on her by keeping in touch with people, nurturing relationships with coworkers so they'll think positively of her. "I feel that if I talk with people, they won't talk about me. I used to call people I work with a lot on my car phone just to check in with them on one thing or another. It showed them that I was interested and it built loyalty. I called as many people a day as I could when I was at lower levels. Now it's harder to find time. But it's still important. I try to keep in mind what is special to people, like their children or other family situations. Too often people get to high-level positions and forget to do this." That, according to Larson, is when they open themselves up to personal attacks, because they've created a distance between themselves and others where rumor and incorrect assumptions can replace reality.

Lording

Lording, another strategy for keeping people in "their place," involves using coercive means to get a person to see or do things the lorder's way. This is a desperate tactic used mostly by the relatively powerless. People who tend to lord over others have a strong need for power. However, no one wants to give them much, and they're not sophisticated enough to develop personal power, so they tend to make their way into positions that enable them to use legitimate power over subordinates in illegitimate ways. "Little Napoleons" is one term for those who engage in such behavior.

A senior executive at one of the top medical centers in the United States described her experiences with a lorder. "He resented my connections and wanted to rule me. He told me to be the first person here in the morning and the last to leave. He lied constantly. When my husband died, he accused me of taking advantage of the situation because I wasn't around when he supposedly needed me. He put me down in front of others constantly. He was just vicious. Anyone who questioned his decisions had to leave. Eventually I did too. It was awful."

Lorders often self-destruct. They wind up making so many enemies that their time in power is self-limiting. There are times, however, when more senior people who know how to manage the lorder want to keep him in place. They know he's incompetent, but they like the way he keeps people in line and away from their doors. This reciprocal arrangement keeps the lorder in power over the less fortunate for longer than is typical for someone with such meager credentials.[3]

The best way to handle lording types is to find a way to sidestep their control. Whatever resource they allocate, find another way to obtain it or learn to operate without it. For example, if the lorder is in charge of computer maintenance, find another channel for getting your computers repaired. If it's your budget, you might need to go over the lorder's head to get the support of his or her boss. It's only your need or desire to receive something from a lorder that enables him or her to have any power over you. Take away the power to make you miserable, and usually you have checked if not checkmated a lorder's political clout.

Giving Them Enough Rope to Hang Themselves

No doubt you've heard people talk at length about some problem, going on and on about why such and such happened and who is at fault, only to finally make things worse for themselves. Often they hoist themselves on their own petard by accidentally admitting to responsibility for the problem, or simply wind up looking petty and vindictive. In such cases, the more people talk, the deeper into trouble they usually get. When someone goes on like this, the politically savvy strategy is to just listen quietly or even inject an encouraging "Please go on" until the individual incriminates himself.

Oftentimes giving people enough rope to hang themselves is not about talk, but behavior. The perpetrator is allowed to continue engaging in some questionable activity until, inevitably, the wrong person finds out.

This strategy works particularly well with compulsively devious people. Eventually, they won't be able to keep up their charade. Sooner or later the holes in their arguments or character begin to appear. The difficulty is in restraining yourself long enough for them to take rope sufficient to the task. Sure, it's tempting to go after them, but if you know they're on a weak track, it often pays to let them self-destruct. On the other hand, some people are such masters of deviousness that you may find yourself hung out to dry before they get there. The "give them enough rope" strategy works best when they're close to putting it around their necks. A little more and they're history. It's not pretty, but it's sometimes necessary.

On the flip side, you need to be careful not to get yourself into such a noose. That's why talking less, and listening and thinking more, are always important.

The Frozen-Out Scenario

Most companies prefer not to fire people if they can get them to leave of their own accord. One way to accomplish this is via isolation, often by putting the targeted person on a low-priority project. In some cases, people are sent to a corporate Siberia by putting them in charge of areas without budgets. The company senior executives hope that by sending a nonverbal message that such people aren't wanted, they will leave on their own accord, sparing the company any risk of a wrongful-termination lawsuit.

The isolation tactic is also applied when someone just doesn't fit. Management may have nothing to do with the decision to edge the person out—his or her peers take it upon themselves to achieve that goal. They keep the person out of the loop, and soon he or she is missing informative lunch talk and even important meetings. Since most people have a need for inclusion, this can be a very cruel but effective way of letting people know that they'd better change their behavior or go elsewhere.

I observed this technique while assisting a company in training employees to more effectively share information and address complaints. In one particularly cohesive division where employees worked tirelessly to bring in profits and were usually successful, the CEO had detected a problematic habit. This division was hoarding information. Other divisions that could have benefited from their expertise were shut out. Anyone in the highly profitable division who was discovered to have shared information with other areas was ostracized until he or she learned his or her lesson. The CEO wanted to break this pattern. Changes in the reward system to encourage information sharing had helped to a degree, but the information hoarding remained firmly in place in this one division. Unless endorsed by the division manager, information sharing would result in the offender being cut out of the loop socially and in terms of new information. It rarely took long for offenders to get the message.

To rectify this situation, the senior executive team and I developed a communication program designed to give people with information or concerns about their inability to provide such information access to people above their managers. Each division met with me to discuss the difficulties in implementing such a program. Eventually, enough managers bought into the process and put enough pressure on the manager who was hoarding information that channels began to open. The CEO met privately with the reluctant manager. He praised her division's success and made clear to her that it was being noticed. He solicited her assistance in training meetings. He began to keep her in the loop in terms of what was going on at higher levels and connected her promotions and those of all managers to efforts made to benefit the entire company. He asked to borrow her people to help in other divisions and praised her for her cooperation. In time, the manager saw that the CEO was holding up her division as a model and that hoarding information was going to hurt her career, whereas sharing it was going to enhance it.

Fake Left, Go Right

This deceitful, manipulative strategy involves allowing or encouraging someone to think one condition exists when in reality another condition holds. Companies have been known to do this by sending a manager out for training when they really plan to get rid of him or her (sometimes referred to as being sent to "bad manager school"). Good managers return from training sessions to find things the way they were. Bad-manager-school candidates return to find that things have changed. They've been fired, demoted, or placed "on special assignment."

Unfortunately, coaching is sometimes used the same way. As a management coach, I've occasionally found myself in situations where the person I'm to coach is unsure whether my arrival is a gift or a signal that the time has come to update his or her résumé. When executives use coaching to improve someone's managerial competence, everyone is well served. When they use it in order to be able to say later, "We tried to help him but nothing worked," no one is served. In addition, the people who remain behind see that the company was deceitful in dealing with a fellow colleague. They begin to wonder who's next.

Tactically handling situations where what is said is not what is meant often requires going over the head of the person who is managing you out of a job, to those who can provide some protection. That's another reason why when you're politically savvy you don't wait until the boom's being lowered before trying to develop helpful relationships. From the outset, you systematically locate and nurture relationships that can be called upon in times of need. Moreover, when others know you're friendly with people in high places, it often has the marvelous effect of steering would-be denigrators away from you. As the saying goes, an ounce of prevention is worth a pound of cure. If you don't have friends in high places, there's no time like the present to begin cultivating them.

Poisoning the Well

According to anthropologist Margaret Mead, people all over the world gossip not only to learn about others but also to raise their own positions in the social sphere. Gossip allows us to lower others and thus raise ourselves.[4] Often done in a manner that makes the negative intentions of the gossiper deniable, this game is a particularly sinister and subtle one. The gossiper may casually drop a derogatory comment about someone into a conversation, or quote someone out of context. "I'm very fond of Pam. I don't know why so many people dislike her. It's a mystery" is the kind of thing a well-poisoner might say.

Sherry Nelson, senior vice-president of a leading aerospace company, recounted this well-poisoning experience to me. "While on maternity leave, I put a manager in my job. When I came back six months later, she'd poisoned the well with some people. Fortunately, I had enough allies to prevent further damage. I went to see her and said, 'I just want you to know that I know exactly what you've done. If you think it will work, you're wrong. I got you this job. You should know that I tried to help you and this isn't going to work.' She naturally denied everything. But I'd put her on notice."

Nelson took a Logical/Commanding approach in this case. She explained why well-poisoning in the future wouldn't work and let the poisoner know that she'd be watching her. An Inspirational might have focused on how such actions undermine the entire team effort: "Your actions not only hurt the person you're attacking but everyone here." A Supportive approach would focus on harm brought to the relationship: "I was very hurt by your attacks. I thought we'd developed a relationship of mutual regard." For a Commanding person this latter approach would be too weak-kneed, an Inspirational would think it too self-focused, and a Logical would find it bereft of persuasive reasoning. The best response is one that suits your style while making clear to the well-poisoner not only that you have recognized her tactics but that you will not sit quietly by if she continues. The latter part can be achieved in the Commanding manner Nelson used or in one of the following ways:

> *Inspirational:* "I may let what you did pass this one time for the benefit of the team."
>
> *Supportive:* "I expect in the future you'll put our relationship first and foremost in your mind."
>
> *Logical:* "I've given this incident considerable thought and it won't be possible for me to sit idly by if it happens again."

Well-poisoning can do you the most harm among those who can promote or fire you. One way to protect yourself is to have friends in the know who'll keep you informed of possible dangers. If you've developed good relationships with these people, you should have a cushion of sorts from any negative information they may receive about you. Psychologists call this cushion "idiosyncrasy credits."[5] These are goodwill credits you've stored up that can save you when a well-poisoner targets you. The people with whom you've built the credits ignore the attacks on you or come to your defense.

If caught early enough, well-poisoning can often be counteracted by a strategy called inoculation. Let others know that you're aware of the previous attempts by an individual to discredit you. Having been so apprised, they may receive future comments of this nature with a degree of skepticism. Have friends speak up for you at any subsequent well-poisoning attempts. This should thwart the poisoner's efforts or at least diminish the negative impact. Let people in high places know of the well-poisonings. Rather than complain endlessly about the situation, ask them if they've ever had a similar experience. Ask them what they did about it. If they get sufficiently interested or concerned, they may provide you with valuable advice or perhaps intervene on your behalf.

Playing It Fast and Loose

People who use this strategy always side with whoever is likely to do them the most good. One day they seem to be your friend, and the next day they act as if they've never met you before. People who make a habit of this tactic are politically dangerous. They usually consider themselves crafty. They have only one loyalty and that is to themselves. But they appear to care about whomever they believe to be of use to them at the time.

After a while, you can spot such people. They change their spots, so to speak, sufficiently often that others begin to distrust them. People who are so good at this strategy that no one realizes their motivations until it's too late are a kind of double agent. They move quickly and unpredictably, so you're never sure whether what you think they may have intended to do was merely accidental. Just when you're on your guard against them, they do some extremely generous thing that forces you to reconsider your protective instincts. It's hard to totally dislike such people because they are helpful when it serves their purposes. Nonetheless, it's important to avoid ever having to rely on them.

The fast-and-loose player will let you believe that you have a deal because he's never said you don't. Of course he's never said you did have a deal either. He might let you get so invested in an endeavor that when he does get around to mentioning that what you thought was the original deal never really existed in his mind (and that he'll need to give you less than you expected), you'll agree to meet his terms. Fast-and-loose people keep their options open until the last minute because they just might want to exit quickly. They're often charming, so it takes a while to detect them. This strategy can come home to roost, of course. The truly adept fast-and-loose don't stay around in one place long enough for that to happen.

If you don't want to be victimized by the fast-and-loose among us, you may have to be a little fast and loose yourself. This meet-fire-with-fire strategy can be very effective. You should never be completely open and honest with a conniving type. Give them as little valuable information as possible. Appear cooperative. Occasionally feign a true interest in their well-being. Praise their accomplishments and don't try to change them. People who are fast and loose are not about to change just to please you. It's a deeply embedded personality characteristic that only they can change by consciously deciding to do so. Your best strategy is to keep a good distance between yourself and them. Otherwise there's a good chance that one day they'll sell your career down the river to advance theirs.

9.

Creating Positional Power

———■———

It's tempting to see power as a trait or title that a person either has or doesn't have. This view of power is very limiting. Power is not an owned entity; rather it emerges through the interactions of people.

Those who achieve the secret handshake realize that what appears power neutral in normal working life, those taken-for-granted "way things are" conditions such as arrangements of desks and chairs in offices, provides subtle ways of signaling who has more power.[1] Messages of power emanate from people as well. Author and power expert Michel Foucault described how power "seeps into the very grain of individuals," reaching into their bodies, where it "permeates their gestures, their posture, what they wear, how they learn to live and work with other people."[2]

Power is so deeply embedded in most daily interactions, so normalized, that only the most astute observers notice the frequency and impact of its presence. It is one thing to be a good observer of power, however, and another to recognize that each person, including you, has the option to accept or reject power allocations.

Even when people do notice the workings of power, they often choose to defer to it. In such cases, the power that one person holds over another exists solely because the person who appears less powerful fears doing anything to alter the balance. Communication expert Klaus Krippendorff points out in his writings that people often get trapped in perceptions of power balances which they could change if they realized that power is not an object, but relationally defined.[3]

If, for example, you believe that you have been patronized by a colleague, but say nothing to this person to discourage future patronizing interactions, then you have reinforced that person's view that he or she has power over you. If you bring the insult to the fore by saying, "That comment was patronizing" or "Don't patronize me," you make the entire interaction accessible for debate and thereby open up the possibility of revision.

The view that power is negotiable is a very liberating one. "Language is the initiator and interpreter of power relations," as linguist Robin Lakoff wrote.[4] If you learn to use language effectively, you become the arbiter of your own power. There's no doubt that your boss or the CEO of your company, or the chairman of the board if you're the CEO, has power over you if you want to keep your job. But were you simply to decide that you could easily get another good job or open a business of your own, then his or her power would be significantly diminished. In fact, if such were the case, you would feel more comfortable talking openly with this person at a company party because there would be less at stake for you should you do or say the wrong thing. This attitude is very liberating.

The Power in Perception

A significant aspect of power, then, lies in perceiving that you have it or could get more of it with a little effort. Even in the midst of dysfunctional organizational politics, you can survive and even thrive if you define your role in a way that does not leave you as a victim. Consider, for example, Socrates when he was on trial in Athens for impiety and corrupting the youth there by sophistry (i.e., charging them money to teach them how to persuade) and dissuading them from listening to their parents. Socrates defended his innocence and even defined the Athenians' irritation with him as a higher calling of sorts:

> *God has appointed me to this city, as though it were a large thoroughbred horse which because of its great size is inclined to be lazy and needs the stimulation of some stinging fly [or gadfly]. It seems to me that God has attached me to this city to perform the office of such a fly; and all day long I never cease to settle here, there, and everywhere, rousing, persuading, reproving every one of you. You will not easily find another like me, gentlemen, and if you take my advice you will spare my life. I suspect, however, that before long you will awake from your drowsing, and in your annoyance you will take Anytus' advice and finish me off with a single slap; and then you will go on sleeping till the end of your days, unless God in his care for you sends someone to take my place.[5]*

While this may seem rather conceited, Socrates shifted the distribution of power between himself and his accusers, frustrating them with his unwillingness to beg for his life and thus give them power.

You may be thinking, "Well, that's all well and good, but they *did* kill him!" Socrates, though, had the power to save himself by apologizing and promising to become someone other than who he was.

This ancient example makes a powerful case that power is not owned, but is created in the processes of perceiving and relating to others. *You do have power, even if it doesn't seem that way at times.* One of the last things you want to make a permanent state in your life is the feeling of powerlessness. Indeed, powerlessness can corrupt as inevitably as power. As Rosabeth Moss Kanter, Harvard professor and business expert, says, "It is powerlessness that often creates ineffective, desultory management and petty, dictatorial, rules-minded managerial styles."[6] It's important to develop your own power or to create a self-defining sense of it. Athletes, artists, and people in other fields sometimes refer to this sense of personal power as being "centered." The centered person draws power from knowing his or her own competencies, being comfortable with those, and refusing to let others diminish them.

Positional and Personal Power

There are two primary types of power: positional and personal. Positional power has to do with how much formal power people perceive you to have. Status, visibility, centrality, relevance, job cachet, and autonomy are a few common forms of positional power. Personal forms of power have to do with traits and styles of acting, such as charisma, dedication, ingratiation, and professionalism. The rest of this chapter will focus on positional power, and chapter 10 will be devoted to personal power.

Manipulating Symbols

Look around any organization and you'll see symbols that convey how those running it want it to be perceived in terms of power. When I visited a friend at a West Coast firm, I entered the building to find that the many banks of elevators didn't seem to have indicators of the floors to which they'd take you. Nor was there a display board of office locations to which I might refer. I wandered about the lobby with several other people, including a lost mail courier. After a while, we noticed that some people waiting for elevators seemed to be staring at the floor. We looked down to find, embedded in the granite floor, the numbers indicating which floors each elevator stopped at.

I finally reached my friend's floor only to experience a continued sense of displacement in the cool, uninviting reception area. I asked the formally dressed receptionist where I could find the rest room, and she directed me down a wide, austere corridor where each door looked just like the other. The rest room itself was marked by a tiny set of easily missed letters. The overwhelming impression was that if you belonged there, you'd know your way around.

The concept of "user-friendly" either had not crossed the architect's mind or more likely had been purposely avoided in order to create an austere environment suited to the practice of powerful business law. The building seemed to say: "We are understated here because we don't need to be otherwise. We have power, class, distinction, distance, and coolness. We are very important. If you were truly rich or important, we would have met you in the lobby. So state your business and be gone." It was a very uncomfortable place, the kind that makes you want to spill something.

A great deal of time and money is poured into making buildings and offices send messages consistent with a company's view of itself. Similarly, smart executives spend a good deal of time thinking about how their offices should be arranged, as well as at least some of the surroundings of those people who work for them. Some people want a desk between you and them to assure that their power is evident. Others prefer to walk from around the desk to sit with you so that you are relaxed and impressed with their welcoming demeanor. Each of these choices sends a message of power distribution.

We all know that verbal and nonverbal symbols and behaviors also convey power. Who wears what, who provides more eye contact, who listens to whom, who dominates, who demurs, who stays late, who leaves early, who speaks louder, who stands close to whom, who touches whom, and who closes their door or, for that matter, who has a door. These are just a few of the many ways that power is conveyed symbolically.

Managing Access

Considerable power in organizations comes from access to people, events, and conversations. This is why rules exist to keep some people out and let others in. Stan Deetz, professor of organizational communication at the University of Colorado, describes how rules limit access to expression outlets. For example, rules can control the types of messages in reports and newsletters, determine who may speak to whom about what, who defers to whom in meetings and other forums, who may express criticism, establish agendas, distribute information, and so forth.[7] Even the use of different forms of address—first names for subordinates and titles and last names for higher management—symbolically sets up barriers that inhibit access of the lower to the higher.

The ways people speak to each other send signals indicative of position on the status hierarchy of organizations. Speech rules keep people "in their place" unless they decide not to be kept there. The prevalence of one-down statements among subordinates tends to discourage them from aggressively gaining access where they may not be wanted. Subordinates are usually expected to use more one-down statements than supervisors, who use more one-up statements.

There are also types of questions that may be asked of superiors and types of invitations that may be proffered. For example, junior managers don't commonly invite CEOs to carpool. It's important to look around the environment in which you work. What are the access rules? How might you circumvent them? If you can't carpool with a senior executive who might help you make a positive career move, what can you do? How have others gained access? These few questions might open up possibilities for you to gain access where it had previously been prohibited.

How to Increase Your Positional Power

Working with the owners of a thriving entrepreneurial venture, I was confronted by the classic issue of respect versus status. The CEO explained to me that he felt that he was not being accorded the respect due him by virtue of his status. As CEO, he believed he should send messages to his direct reports via e-mail and that they should respond immediately. When they didn't do so, he was indignant. "Why aren't they responding?" he asked me. "Shouldn't they put my requests above all others?"

In an autocracy they would. But most organizations are places where power is managed and respect goes to those who manage it well. Mark Day, senior executive at a Los Angeles–based defense company where I've spent a good deal of consulting time, believes "there is power that comes from holding a higher position and there is power that comes from respect. I'd much rather have the respect type," he says. "I've seen supervisors with authoritative power alone get only what they ask for from people. Consequently, they have to expend much more energy to accomplish their work because they have to think of every move their people will make. Supervisors with respect find that people offer to do more and take on more responsibility, which in turn lightens the management load."

As for the CEO who believed he was not getting enough respect, I advised him to become less reliant on e-mail. As a rule, it should be used only for information that is quick and not open to interpretation. I suggested he walk around more, talk with people about what he and they care about, give directions face-to-face whenever possible, and be responsive to others' input. The CEO or manager who won't get out of his or her chair to talk with people loses a lot of information and respect.

This CEO also needed to recognize the distinction between authority and respect; the former rarely lasts long without the latter. Respect comes to those who listen to other people, deliberate and even change their views if a better suggestion comes along. It's earned. It also comes to those who express appreciation face-to-face, who find the time to say, "Nice job," "That's a great idea," or "I'm glad I stopped by to talk with you. I need to do it more often."

The Power of Relevance

Relevance is a way to develop power based on what you do. If your job and skills match with the priorities of the company, then you are more relevant than those who are less well matched. While it's true that an R&D vice-president is very important to a high-tech firm, so are the resident systems troubleshooter and the plant maintenance worker if the problem at hand is up their alley.

Relevance isn't a static trait. There are ways to improve your relevance. You can develop your skills to make them more salient to your company or focus your efforts on earnings-driving tasks. By increasing your relevance, you increase your personal clout. But you need to be sure you know what counts to the organization before investing your time and effort. You also need to know what matters to you and where you might use your skill in a more relevant manner, if it's not possible to do so in your current job.

William Dahlman, CEO of Employers Group, a human resources information, consulting, training, and electronic support organization serving over five thousand California employers, offers this advice: "You can break through by making something work better or more efficiently. That's how computer geeks get into show business. Also, people who share the pain in rough times, those who offer advice or question a policy in a politically astute way, add value." Dahlman believes that people often neglect to notice that their bosses are dealing with inherited politics. The ones who do notice and who help their superiors work through the difficulties are, Dahlman says, "likely to be noticed."

Everyone I interviewed for this book feels that he or she has succeeded by doing these kinds of things. The following list provides some ways these businesspeople increased their relevance. They might prove useful to you as well.

1. Identify your educational or skill gaps and get training either through or outside the company.
2. Find yourself a good coach or mentor who can assist you in identifying what it would take for you to become more relevant. Work with him or her on improving your skills.
3. Connect with well-respected people in the organization whose areas are considered highly relevant. Identify skills you have that might be useful to them. Offer to help.
4. Look around to see what's missing on the teams of which you're a member, or ones you might join. There are team roles (initiator, critic, elaborator, idea generator, recorder, conflict manager, and, perhaps most important, follow-up) that groups need in order to function effectively. Identify where the team is lacking, where you could effectively fit in, and take on that role.

The Power of Centrality

Centrality is a form of power that accrues from occupying central positions in important networks. People in more peripheral positions must depend on such persons for information. To the extent that information must flow through you to get to others who need it, you are in a central position. You are a conduit for information. This ensures people's dependence on you and so increases your power. As mentioned earlier, it isn't that the power resides in the central position but that people perceive you as integral and relate to you in ways that give you power. Centrality relies on ~~making~~ yourself a key link in the information chain.

Even a CEO can become peripheral rather than central if he or she drops out of the chain of information. I've seen CEOs become so enamored with their other roles that they remove themselves as an information link. Jack Welch of GE, on the other hand, constantly visits GE businesses and meets with partners and potential partners. He spends weeks at a time meeting with managers in Europe and Asia. At each location he encourages workers to speak out. He maintains himself as a conduit and expects others to act as Conduits too.[8]

You don't need to be a CEO to be central. To make yourself central, the first thing you must do is recognize that you *can* be central. Then you need to start obtaining a flow of important information. Pass it along to people for whom it is relevant. Once people depend on you for information, you're on your way to increased centrality.

Part of centrality is physical location. Out-of-the-way offices not only keep people out of the flow of information but also often symbolize that the occupant's work is peripheral to the organization. If you can't change a remote office location, it's wise to leave it occasionally and gravitate to where the action is. Don't do everything via phone or e-mail. Drop in with information, make lunch dates to discuss important issues, deliver an opinion in person. If you want to increase your centrality, it's wise to take note of or find out where rising stars, solid performers, and the people with information or status tend to congregate. Then be sure to be there when they are. This is the best way to be "in the right place at the right time."

The Power of Career Cachet

"Career cachet" refers to the potential power benefit you derive from being in an appreciated occupation. Let's face it: Some jobs carry stigmas. A successful venture capitalist told me, "I've never taken jobs that start with the letter 'P,' like public relations and personnel." Another executive said, "I want to be where the money's coming in, not where it's going out." These are broad, sweeping statements, and they may not be at all applicable in your own situation, but they make the valid point that some jobs won't be effective at helping you get into the inner circle. This is partly because people are inclined to make "us"-versus-"them" distinctions.

Organizational behavior expert Karl Weick says that certain job types become esteemed and others disparaged as ideological systems emerge to help make sense of the multiple and often conflicting interpretations of reality that we find in organizational life.[9] Many of these ideologies are self-serving; they maintain or increase the prestige of the people who developed them. Nevertheless, consensus eventually develops around certain ideologies, sustaining the belief that some specialties are superior—even when there ceases to be, or indeed never was, any factual reason to support that perspective.

What should you do if upon assessing your position, you realize that it lacks the cachet needed for advancement in your company? You could work hard and wait until your job becomes more appreciated. But the faster means by which people create or maintain prestige for themselves is by differentiating what they do from the tasks normally associated with their devalued occupation. You might want to seek a transfer or change in job description that will affiliate you at least partially with tasks that enjoy higher status. To do this requires an astute assessment of what activities are in and out of favor, and likely to be so for the foreseeable future.

If you have low career cachet and you're lucky, it might just be a matter of waiting until others realize that the areas they've been disparaging are actually quite valuable. When the wait looks too long, you can do what many secret handshake holders have done: take a pay cut if necessary and go work in a division that is better appreciated and where people advance more rapidly.

The Power of Autonomy

Autonomy is an aspect of power that has to do with having the discretion, or freedom, to exercise your judgment on the job. Autonomy indicates that the people for whom you work trust you.

Some people derive autonomy from their title. Linda Hill, in her article "Power Dynamics in Organizations," points to how newly minted M.B.A.'s are often attracted to "assistant to the president" positions because they'll be sent off without much guidance to do a variety of assignments.[10] Some of them are likely to be of strategic importance. If they do well, not only do they become autonomous but their relevance power increases as well. The senior executive starts to rely on them more and more and soon they're indispensable. Assistant to the president jobs aren't the only ones where this kind of increasing autonomy and indispensability can be achieved. Some jobs come with autonomy. Consultants achieve this, as do entrepreneurs. They often give autonomy to the people they hire because they value it themselves.

Companies vary considerably in the extent to which they provide autonomy to workers. Some companies are empowering types: They want you to stop the engines if you think they're going off the track. They don't even mind if a talented person comes up with an idea that doesn't work, so long as he or she comes up with ideas that work much of the time. There's room for failure in such companies and so there's room for autonomy.

Beth Berke, executive vice president and chief administrative officer at Sony Pictures Entertainment, says that almost anyone can have autonomy. They just have to be willing to step up and seize the opportunity, as long as they are equally willing to take the accompanying responsibility. What's difficult, she told me, is training someone to take initiative who isn't inclined to do so. "You can always pull someone back," Berke said, "by telling them, 'Next time check with me before you do something like that,' but it's harder to make someone take risks who isn't inclined to do so."

Berke told me about a pivotal moment in her career. As a production lawyer, she watched a woman make a key deal with an actor. Throughout the meeting, the deal maker was writing furiously on her pad. Occasionally, she paused to ask a question. Then she made an offer. The actor took it. Afterward, Berke asked the deal maker how she'd come to the offer amount. Thinking there was some "Holy Grail system," she even asked to see her colleague's notes. On the pad was doodling, nothing more. That taught Berke that there's rarely a magic formula for making the right decisions. Instead, you need to have confidence in what you're doing and be willing to step up, take a chance, and take a hit if you're wrong.

Here are a few ways that you might use to increase your autonomy:

1. Look carefully at your present job. Do you have enough autonomy? If not, is it because your boss micromanages? Is it because you haven't established a track record of autonomy? If the boss is an incurable micromanager, you may need to find ways to work on projects he or she does not oversee. If it's your track record, why not talk to the boss about achieving one? Ask him or her to give you a chance and then make sure you come through. Start small.

2. Establish trust. Make sure you do what you say you'll do and do it well when someone does give you autonomy. There may not be a second chance.

3. Don't always ask permission, especially on the smaller stuff. If the downside is not significant, take some initiative on tasks where it isn't clear that you should ask permission.

4. Create jobs on which you can demonstrate autonomy. If you can't get out from under someone's micromanaging style on assignments he or she has given you, do so on ones you create yourself.

5. Add value. This is key in achieving autonomy. Go a step further than others in getting a job done well. People like this don't need constant supervision.

While attempting to achieve greater autonomy, it's always possible to go down the wrong path. In general, follow the advice of General George Patton—a good plan violently executed today is better than an excellent plan tomorrow. Make sure you've done your homework, then ask yourself if you're confident that what you're planning will work. If so, go for it. And while autonomy means accomplishing things on your own, it's always wise to give credit to those who help you out.

The Power of Visibility

Bill Davidson, founding partner and chairman of Redrock Capital LLC, an investment and consulting group focusing on emerging growth companies, believes "the best way to pursue your own interests is to *visibly* put the company's interests first. Let them know you're a player, not a groupie." What keeps many people from doing this? "Most people have narrow definitions of their self-interests and so fail to broaden and connect them to those of the company."

Davidson isn't talking about being someone other than who you are, but rather looking at what you want and what the company wants and finding a connection. Sometimes that means making a statement about the career risks you'll take to do what's best for the company.

Venture capitalist Tania Modic did this at a young age. In her first job out of college, she was an assistant marketing development officer at a bank. She had a nice title, but there was one catch: There was no marketing development officer for Modic to assist. She was a glorified research assistant, reporting to lots of people and doing a lot of what she calls "dog work." She wanted to move over to the bank's lending operations and become an account officer, but so did everyone else. So Modic took action. Using her vacation time and her own money to travel to New York City, she called on a number of accounts that she knew were being ignored by account officers at the bank. Some of these accounts hadn't been called on in years! By the time Modic completed her New York trip, she'd personally corralled several valuable heretofore lost accounts. Upon her return some account officers' noses were out of joint, but the senior people with whom she'd begun to nurture relationships were impressed.

Modic then took another bold step. On a Friday evening, when most people had gone home for the weekend, she picked up a phone call that turned out to be the CEO of a large Texas company, whose business the bank had for years been trying to obtain without success. The CEO disclosed to Modic that his company was in a difficult situation and needed a large loan. Modic asked him what amount his current banks were willing to provide. He said they were willing to lend him up to $20 million. The CEO asked, "So, can you guys help?" Modic's ceiling for approving loans was $1 million, but she approved a $20-million loan on the spot. Monday morning, the young banker had a great deal of explaining to do. But after the dust settled, she received a brilliant performance review. She told me that the only negative comment on her appraisal that year was, "She tends to exceed her authority."

Often, developing your visibility is simply a matter of identifying the "hot" tasks or projects and then going after them. Ask which tasks keep you scurrying about meeting the same people, and which ones open new doors. Go for the latter.

Barbara Jean, co-owner of The Competitive Edge, a management consulting company, rose through the ranks at Kodak by refusing to wait to see whether or not she'd be chosen for a job. Instead, she'd go ahead and ask for it. "Sometimes they'd say no, but that didn't matter," Jean recalls, "because after a while, they got so tired of saying no that they would say yes."

However, David Carpenter, CEO of UniHealth, whom we met in chapter 6, cautions that the common wisdom about asking for a job is a bit overrated. When people are focused more on getting ahead than doing their job well, Carpenter says they don't go far. "Today the most overlooked way to get noticed is to perform at an excellent level in what you're doing at the time. Most CEOs are smarter than you might think and they notice such people. Don't look solely to the next promotion. Mind the p's and q's at the point you're at. In doing so, you'll get noticed." Carpenter told me of a time when he walked up to a CEO and asked him why he had chosen a particular candidate over many others for a high-level post. The reply: "He was the only one who really asked for the job." Carpenter explains, "He wasn't talking about walking up and saying, 'Hey, I want this job'; he was referring to how this person not only did his job well but in doing so demonstrated that he had the abilities, the dedication, and the executive maturity necessary to move up."

Visibility has a downside too. Politically speaking, you have to know when to stand out and when to stand down. Don't get desperate for attention, because it shows and it isn't appealing. A little humility is a very good companion to visibility. Watch out for signals of jealousy among your peers. Let someone else enjoy the limelight for a while, and then get back out there when it really counts. The key is to become visible to the right people at the right times.

10.

Enhancing Your Personal Power

———————

Personal power consists of traits and skills that make people influential. As with positional power, personal power consists of several types, each capable of moving you closer to the secret handshake.

The Power of Expertise

You'd think expertise would be a given to hold a position of any responsibility, wouldn't you? But look around with a clear eye and you'll observe—if you haven't already—that such is not at all the case.

Jeffrey Pfeffer and Robert Sutton have described how companies reward people for what they call "smart talk." This kind of talk is "an especially insidious inhibitor of organizational action."[1] It includes sounding confident, articulate, and even eloquent. The people using it may well have good ideas, but two of the less benign components of smart talk are a tendency to make things unnecessarily complicated and/or abstract, and an inclination to be critical and negative. What smart talkers say may sound funny at first and even flattering when they berate others in front of you. But chances are your turn will come as the target of those jokes because the true smart talker is usually all talk at everyone's expense except his or her own.

Closely allied to smart talk is the loudmouth or blabbermouth theory of leadership.[2] This theory holds that persons who talk the loudest or longest—regardless of the quality of their comments—often become leaders of groups. After a while, some people learn that instead of taking risky actions to get ahead, they should just talk loudly and often about what to do.

People eventually recognize smart talkers and loudmouths for what they are. If you want to reach positions of true power and authority, you must have true expertise. However, one of the most difficult challenges for people with considerable expertise is getting past the assumption that just because they have it, other people are going to recognize and respect it. When it comes to getting ahead, the most important thing is to help other people realize how good you are.

Let's start with the premise that few things speak more loudly than results. Given that, you need to ask yourself what the people to whom you report are looking for. Wouldn't it be a breath of fresh air for those to whom you're accountable to see things of value to them actually get done in a timely and competent manner? Pfeffer and Sutton suggest you become one of the people who ask "how" rather than "why" questions. They recommend closing the knowledge-versus-doing gap by making the *doing* of things the standard by which one judges what's right.

Steven Sample, president of USC, knew he wanted to be a university president when he was twenty-nine years of age. When I asked why he thought so early in his career that he could be a successful academic CEO, he shared with me advice that a sage mentor had given him regarding setting oneself apart from other front runners. "He told me that a lot of people want to *be* a university president, but very few want to *do* university president. If you want to reach the inner circles of business, it's important to be a doer."

One way to get noticed as a doer is to identify people in other divisions or at other levels who may have a need for your expertise. As the saying goes, a person is never a prophet in his own country. A colleague gave me a very good piece of advice one time: "I've always believed you should have an audience outside of the one right around you." People who don't have to see you every day—or compete with you at raise and promotion time—are less likely to be threatened by your expertise.

This is why many hard chargers get involved in nonprofit work. Few people listen to them during the day, so they go out and do wonders for volunteer organizations. There they meet other secret handshake holders who support and promote them up the ladder of nonprofit visibility. Soon word of their great deeds gets back to their offices. Working for a nonprofit, philanthropic foundation can be a significant societal contribution and an effective back door to visibility and recognition of your expertise.

The Power of Dedication

Another way that people who otherwise would not have power are able to obtain it is by demonstrating dedication to their company.

At a training session I was providing on the topic of leadership, a manager raised his hand to tell me about how he needed help one night with a new technology. It was 11 P.M., but leaving the question unanswered might have caused significant delay. His liaison, John, at Cisco Systems, from whom the part had been purchased, had given him a telephone number. John had said that the number could be called anytime day or night. So the manager dialed the number and, sure enough, John picked up the phone and was glad to be of help.

Being dedicated doesn't necessarily mean putting in long hours or being constantly available. To the contrary, it's important to put in long hours and be available when it matters to those in a position to notice your dedication. Otherwise you're headed for burnout, and your extra effort just becomes expected, rather than the important contribution it really is.

Roy Romer, introduced in chapter 5, demonstrated considerable dedication to expansion of the Denver, Colorado, airport when he was governor. Residents of nearby Adams County were concerned about the annexing of land there for a new runway as well as about increased noise. Romer decided to go on what became known as "the oatmeal circuit." He told a dubious press that every morning for sixty days he would have oatmeal breakfasts with the residents of Adams County at three different times in three different restaurants. He promised to begin the breakfasts at 5:30 A.M. and he lived up to the promise. He wore a leather jacket rather than a suit and tie and talked with anyone who cared to show up. "One woman whose chickens were at the end of the proposed runway needed to talk," Romer told me. She got his undivided attention. So did each breakfast companion. He explained to each of them the benefits that would accrue were they to support the airport expansion. "The symbolism was key here," Romer said referring to the casual jacket, time commitment, and heart-to-heart nature of the breakfast interactions. "I was joining them where they stood and talking about what mattered to them."

Romer's dedication was made obvious, in part, by the number of days he chose to demonstrate it. Three breakfasts every morning for sixty days is no small promise. There is a version of dedication that says, "no pain, no gain." In such companies, dedication may be the willingness to take a transfer that will bring you and your family considerable discomfort. Or it could be a willingness to spend much of the year on the road. A certain amount of such "dedication" is normal, and, politically speaking, it can be very effective. Nevertheless, it's counterproductive to take such an attitude to the extreme. Some people lose perspective when they spend so much of their time traveling, for instance. They fail to realize that a well-planned conference call might work just as well as another trip. Besides, being out of sight *too* often is a good way to be out of your boss's mind when promotion time comes around.

On a related note, people in many companies use the appearance of busyness to increase their personal power. They frantically scurry up and down hallways, speak quickly, and look harried during phone calls. At such "high-energy shops," if you don't run around like you're on the verge of a nervous breakdown, they may not think you are appropriately dedicated. Frankly, however, those in the inner circle of most companies are not looking to invite in Nervous Nellie and Jittery Jack, but rather people who can be highly productive while remaining poised, clearheaded, and objective at the same time.

Being willing to get your hands dirty is another way to demonstrate dedication. This can mean relieving your boss of tasks that he or she finds worrisome or distasteful. We all have things we don't like to do.

Some people dislike writing speeches, hate entering social gatherings, or fear embarrassing themselves by forgetting names. Consider how you might be of assistance. Perhaps you're a crackerjack writer, a Don Juan of introductions, or blessed with a steel-trap memory for names. Again, be sure the helpful task you take on is visible and valued.

Pay attention to the signs of dedication that appear important to your superiors. Some CEOs believe so strongly in always putting in extra hours that if you go home at the normal quitting time, they think you're doing a poor job. Does that mean that if you work late every night you're necessarily more dedicated or do a better job than others? Of course not, but it's the message you have to worry about.

Creating a Positive Impression

We've all met people with charisma. They walk into a room and heads turn. People surround them and seek their attention. Charles Handy, author, management consultant, and former professor at the London Business School, proposes that managers must be proactive in the management of their careers and in how they are perceived. Perhaps charisma is a tall order, but all of us can increase the likelihood of being perceived in a positive light. The responsibility for this is our own. As Charles Handy explains, "In a world of skill-related earnings it is of little use relying on the village of elders to nurture and guide your upbringing." It is increasingly the responsibility of each manager to package and promote himself. In his book *Understanding Organizations*, Handy suggests that managers develop themselves in ways that adhere to the interests, truths, or what he calls "fashions" of the cultures in which they work. It's imperative to nurture and guide one's own upbringing and also to "alter or boost skills" that will be appreciated, "to find the right market for those skills and to sell them to the appropriate buyer." This requires an avoidance of predictability and stagnation, a flexibility of impression formation that enhances the likelihood of being noticed and therefore promoted.[3]

Stretching the Envelope

It was Machiavelli who reasoned that "everybody sees what you appear to be, few feel what you are."[4] People with charisma are masters of managing perceptions. They know as Machiavelli did that impressions are more powerful and accessible than reality. If people took the time to study each other, to really know whom they're dealing with, and if we didn't spend so much of our days engaged in "tact," dressing down when others dress up would pose no problem. But we don't have time to study each other. So we emphasize our best qualities when it truly matters. Wearing a "power suit" to an interview, for example, doesn't mean you won't be nervous, yet it may well convey more composure and self-confidence than you really have. It presents you in a positive light and helps to make you memorable. The suit is not so much a lie about who you are as a slight exaggeration. Since everyone else is exaggerating in this way too, not to do so decreases your likelihood of getting the job.

Impression management is a personal power tactic. An organized office and consistent punctuality can convey the impression that a person has an organized mind. Good grooming and tasteful clothing suggest confidence and pride. Walking briskly and looking busy but not harried, especially in times of stress, can convey capability. Humor under such conditions indicates charm and composure.

It's even important to notice what the heavy hitters are wearing, how their voices sound, when they speak and for how long, with what amount of humor, and the many other ways they go about impressing people.

Theresa Ravese Blinder, vice-president, finance, for Unilever's Detergents and Household Care Business Unit, noticed early in her career that it's important to dress "to optimize, not just to please others." She avoids strong colors like red and purple, she told me, "because my style is already strong." She finds oranges and greens "too playful." She prefers blues, blacks, and browns, which she finds professional and stylish.

Ravese Blinder also noticed that her tendency to speak quickly created an impression of impatience. She began to speak more slowly. She considers this kind of attention to detail a means of enhancing your chances of being discovered. It's one thing to take on tough, visible jobs as she did, but it's quite another to be remembered for doing so. By revising aspects of her style, dress, and demeanor, she increased the likelihood that her contributions would not pass unnoticed.

Here again Machiavelli's wisdom comes in handy. He described how nature has given each of us a different face, character, and imagination. But the most successful among us are those who fit their actions "to the times and to the order of things."[5] Impression management is this type of endeavor. Ravese Blinder's success is a testament to the fact that being an astute observer of "the order of things," even in matters of dress and voice, influences the level of one's career success.

If It Walks Like a Duck . . .

Impression management can take the form of copying another's behaviors. This is supposedly one of the sincerest forms of flattery. Mirroring of the boss's behavior by walking and talking like him or her is effective to a point. When the mimicking is not overdone, those being mimicked tend to grant favors to the mimicker, especially if he or she is good at it. Since people tend to be attracted to others who are like themselves, this form of ingratiation can work wonders, distasteful as it is when taken to extremes.

This preference for one's own kind is exactly why organizational diversity is so difficult to achieve. If the people running your organization aren't like you in fundamental ways, you'll have difficulty achieving the secret handshake. One avenue for gaining acceptance and appreciation is cut off unless the people in charge recognize their own biases and seek instead to reward ideas and actions that complement rather than copy their own.

The best advice is, approximate, don't imitate. Walk like the duck, but don't try to be the duck. Cynthia Neff, human relations director at IBM's Watson Research Center, has seen what she calls "overly political" people self-destruct when attempting to please the higher-ups by mimicking them. Their mistake most often lies in their underestimation of the capacity of others to recognize such maneuvers.

Confidence Quotient

Confidence is an aspect of personal power. Yet there's always the risk of overdoing it or even the appearance of overdoing it. One of the CEOs interviewed for this book told me he overstepped his confidence quotient one time. By word of mouth it got back to him after he'd missed a promotion that one of the senior executives had said at the promotion meeting, "I don't like that guy. He's a peacock strutting around." And, this CEO told me, "The guy was probably right." So he toned down his overconfident style and was left with enough confidence to, in a few post-peacock years, work his way to the company's top post.

There's much to be said for a little humility, yet little is said or written about it in business. Ken Blanchard and Norman Vincent Peale in *The Power of Ethical Management* wrote, "People with humility don't think less of themselves, they just think of themselves less." Blanchard explains in his later book *The Heart of a Leader* the dangers in wanting to be center stage all the time. It's an addiction he says. Such people fail to "develop and use people's talents or catch them doing something right. They want to be the best—'the fairest of them all.' " According to Blanchard, "A great rule for business today is: Think more about your people and they will think more of themselves."[6] Let others be in the spotlight.

Phil Slater, author and philosopher, suggests asking whether your ego is tyrannical. When the ego takes over, it attends to matters like getting richer, being the smartest, and looking the best. "The ego says, 'I know we made $100 million but what if all of it goes away? We'd better make another $100 million.' " An ego run amok doesn't even let the body sleep, Slater says. It shoots the messenger by ignoring the body's urgent messages to rest and reflect until finally the body falls ill just to get noticed. This kind of ego, Slater warns, "doesn't recognize the complex system of which it is a part."[7]

Slater believes we're moving into a time when right-brain thinking (emotional, relational) is becoming more important than having the right or most logical answers. Confidence is still key to success, but not if taken to the extreme. The effective leaders of today's organizations are information seekers. They aren't necessarily the ones with the answers; they're the ones who know where to find them. Thomas Davenport, director of the Andersen Consulting Institute for Strategic Change and professor at Boston University, writes of knowledge networks where people with passion for the same kinds of work are brought together to share information. The tyrannical ego won't do that.[8] It's just too risky. Others might get credit and that's not what the tyrannical ego wants.

John Seely Brown, chief scientist of Xerox Corporation and director of its Palo Alto Research Center (PARC), proposes that the organization-hopping characteristic of today's careers makes it likely that people will establish identities not solely within their organizations but within clusters of people with shared interests. Your success, Brown suggests, will depend in part on how well you form an "identity within the structure of your cluster not just your organization."[9] This means that those who are sufficiently "wired in" to key knowledge clusters will have an advantage.

According to Brown, it will also become increasingly important to "learn how to unlearn,"[10] what Sidney Harman, chairman of Harman International Industries, calls "subordinating yourself to the issue at hand rather than insisting on having your perspectives adapted by all." Harman uses a metaphor to clarify this important point: "In a jazz quartet every player is a genius but each adapts to the other."[11] The out-of-control ego can't do this because it refuses to cooperate.

Contrary to the "may the best paradigm win" rule of the past, which dictates that the only way to have an idea take hold is to blast holes in previously favored ones, scaling the heights of knowledge clusters will involve the kind of cooperative political dancing described in chapter 7. Crediting people for their contributions and introducing ideas as extensions of prior thought rather than isolated insights will be the norm.

General Electric under Jack Welch has endeavored to make this kind of sharing the information and the credit the company's norm. Steve Kerr, chief learning officer for GE, describes the mind-set there as one favoring "input, throughput, and output." The goal is information integration, and the key to achieving it is "to respect differences while also finding commonalities."[12] This approach suggests that the kind of confidence needed by those wishing to achieve the secret handshake is one that is not easily threatened, one that welcomes discussion and debate.

Jim O'Toole, research professor at the Center for Effective Organizations and prolific author, says that people likely to reach leadership positions today believe that "the more power you give away, the more you have,"[13] and this applies to information power too. Jean Lipman-Blumen, cofounding director of the Institute for Advanced Studies in Leadership at the Peter F. Drucker Graduate School of Management, says leaders of the future will be people "who want to be where meaning might emerge, the people who refuse to drink continuously from the same information well."[14] And Frances Hesselbein, CEO of Girl Scouts of the U.S.A. and chairwoman of the Peter F. Drucker Foundation for Nonprofit Management, believes that such knowledge and meaning will emerge in the most unlikely places, not just from "people who look like General Schwarzkopf."[15] If you're looking in all the wrong places, including only into your own mind, you'll surely miss out.

It follows, then, that if you wish to be perceived as having what it takes to be a player in the inner circle, you can't hoard information or attempt to give people the impression that you alone have the answers to complex problems. Blasting holes in the ideas of others in order to make your own more visible won't work anymore either. Moreover, according to John Seely Brown, the future will require a bridging across intellectual boundaries, including those of the humanities and science. There will be "no more physics envy," he argues. "Taste and aesthetics" will drive us forward to understand what is now unknown. As Brown sees it, the person who will hold power in the future is the one who can "go beyond the obvious in knowledge to the rich interplay" of heretofore disparate areas of study.

11.

Managing the Micropolitics of Conflict

———■———

You could adopt all of the political skills we've addressed in chapters 1 through 10 and still not achieve the secret handshake if you can't manage conflict. Conflict is inevitable whenever people are working together, but especially if they are also competing. Despite all the talk about teams in business circles today, competition is rewarded more than cooperation, and so conflict is the inevitable result.

Douglas McGregor, one of the forefathers of management theory, described the situation this way: "Our people return from their teambuilding weekends and, within a few days (hours?), they're often back to building their empires at the expense of the other team members and with the hope of a superior (i.e., winning) performance appraisal, higher merit pay, the next promotion, or more job security."[1] While this kind of internal competition squelches creativity and innovation by inhibiting dialogue and wreaking havoc on relationships, it is still a common part of everyday work life.

One of the key skills separating those who reach the inner circles of both large and small, slow and fast businesses from those who fall by the wayside is the ability to manage conflict in a way that encourages creativity and innovation, dialogue and relationship building. It's to this talent that we turn now.

Choose Your Battles

No matter how cooperative your work environment, there will always be opportunities to engage in verbal battle. It's wise, we've all heard, to choose your battles carefully. Unfortunately, this is one of those easier-said-than-done rules of business. Yet it is essential that you master it in order to achieve the secret handshake. The first step on the way to this mastery is to learn how to use the PURRR model introduced in chapter 6: pause, understand, reflect, reinterpret, and redirect.

When your blood begins to boil and you're seething with anger and animosity, that's when a "red flag emotion alert" should go off in your mind. It isn't enough to count to ten. Buy yourself some time by saying: "What you just said [or did] can be interpreted in a variety of ways." See how the other person responds. Often just saying this alerts him or her that battle lines might start being drawn. If he or she doesn't want to do battle, you will have provided an opportunity to avoid it by not reacting harshly or impulsively.

Calling a halt to overt confrontation will often release underlying assumptions and open up avenues of communication that are otherwise closed. Of course, doing so effectively takes a clear understanding of what is going on behind the scenes and skillfulness in bringing it constructively to the fore.

Let's start with language. We've already discussed how the way people frame or position an event influences how others will respond or react. It's also true that the words we use either create conflict or prevent it, depending on the perceptions they foster. No doubt you've been in the situation where you met someone for the first time and you just didn't "connect." On another day, at another time, maybe in another universe, you know that you and she might have. But on that day in that place at that time, you and she did not create perceptions for each other and together that were conducive to feelings of mutual positive regard.

Had one of you been in a slightly different mood or had your brains been functioning at a somewhat higher level allowing one or both of you to select words more carefully or to be more relaxed, things might have gone much better. It's important to recognize when the right words just don't seem to be coming to you. When that happens, it's often best to let the other person know that you aren't at your best. It beats prematurely souring a relationship.

Conflict can also occur when topics are avoided or forms of expression thwarted (real men don't cry and real women don't make trouble). When people feel that expectations regarding status, age, gender, etc., preclude them from saying what they're thinking, issues often can't be adequately resolved.

While it isn't always wise to say the unsayable or unearth that which has been buried, there are times when doing so is necessary to resolve conflict. The truly expert communicator might work to gently expose the underlying reason why two people can't discuss an issue, question whether they should be so constrained, and then move toward an alternative perception and more open communication.

George Mitchell, senator-turned-negotiator, tried to rescue the peace process in Northern Ireland from the brink of collapse in November 1999 by giving both sides a chance to say the unsayable. He ordered a media blackout to facilitate the airing of views and cloistered the parties in the U.S. ambassador's residence in London, away from the media. For two weeks, people who could not stand each other strolled the halls, ate, relaxed, and talked together. Mitchell described it this way: "I insisted there was no assigned seating at dinner, no nationalists on one side, unionists on the other. It was mixed up, random, and there were no negotiations. We talked about sports, family, fishing, things like that. And gradually, the proper atmosphere was created."[2]

When the two sides failed to understand each other, Mitchell asked them questions that needed to be asked. He questioned, in a delicate manner, what had remained unquestioned in their minds for many years. He encouraged them to draft documents they each wanted to have provided by the other side. He essentially broke down the dominant perceptual fields of both sides and worked with them to create one together. They may not have achieved a perfect result, but they achieved one that neither side had envisioned possible prior to the summit.

Politics exists because people promote cherished views. They attempt to silence those with whom they disagree, protecting themselves and their organizations from examination and scrutiny. The more assumptions remain unchecked, the more politicized environments become.

In the midst of constant constraining of what's discussable, it pays to be able to see how you're being limited even if you don't choose to challenge the system. The politically adept even find it useful to occasionally say the unsayable. They do so when the timing seems right—when what has remained unsaid seems to be falling into some disfavor anyway. *Timing is crucial here.*

If you are always the complacent team player who can be counted on to never rock the boat, you'll never make a mark for yourself. Even in cultures where not standing out is prized, knowing when to speak up is crucial. Richard E. Lewis, CEO of the accounting placement service Accountants Overload in West Los Angeles, uses a well-known prayer as a reminder to himself and the people working for him: "God grant me the serenity to accept the things I cannot change, the courage to change the things I can, and the wisdom to know the difference."

Such wisdom is a form of political savvy. Edward Lawler, director of the Center for Effective Organizations at the University of Southern California, terms such advice "knowing when to fold the tent." Lawler offers the following guidelines for determining when a situation isn't worth battling:

1. There's a low probability of winning without doing excessive damage.
2. Upon reflection the importance of winning isn't as high as it originally seemed.
3. There will likely be a time down the line when you can raise the issue again with a different boss or in a different way.

When you feel strongly about something, it's difficult to convince yourself that you'd be better off not pushing to accomplish your goals. But this is where political sophistication pays off.

When M.B.A. students enter their first negotiations in my Negotiation and Persuasion class, many focus on the prize. They want to learn the best tactics—the ones that will cause the other negotiator to say, "Okay, you win." What they often overlook is that in the process of achieving victory, they alienate the other person. In negotiation, even if you win on content level with the best idea, data, or strategy, you can still lose in terms of the relationship. So estimating probabilities of winning means estimating on both dimensions—content and relationship.

A second reason for not pushing through an idea is that upon reflection it may seem less important than it did earlier. Before picking a fight, pause to reflect. Suppose you're about to send a scathing memo to someone by e-mail. All you have to do is hit the reply button. But just because it's easy doesn't mean it's wise.

"Never Try to Teach a Pig to Read"

This bit of wisdom comes from a saying on the door of one of my professors' offices when I was an undergraduate. The words were accompanied by a picture of a pig. The full caption read, "Never try to teach a pig to read. It's a waste of time and it annoys the pig."

It's important to know who can be managed and who cannot. Some people, try as you might to work with them, get more stubborn or adversarial with each attempt. It's important to know the difference between people who are reachable and those who will just waste your time.

Cynthia Neff, human relations director for IBM's Watson Research Center, puts it this way: "You can't dress up a dead moose." If it's dead, it's dead. Many conflicts at work are over issues that have been deceased for a good long time. The skill is in knowing when it's wise to face that fact and move forward, putting the pain behind you. This applies to situations in which someone simply isn't going to change. Instead of putting a lot of effort into creating a miracle, it's often better to find a way to work with these people, to essentially manage them within the constraints of their inadequacies.

Leonard Schlesinger, senior vice-president for development at Brown University, says his first job taught him an important lesson: "Back then I worked for the state government of Rhode Island. My boss was as dumb as a rock. But he required only three things of me. He needed to get credit for everything; he wanted to be fully briefed weekly; and he wanted me to get him into the newspaper as much as I could. If I did these things, I had the latitude to do whatever I wanted with my work."[3]

Everybody wants something. Often you're in a position to give it to them, but you have to find out what it is. There are people, however, who aren't about to change no matter how helpful you are or how gracefully you show them the error of their ways. The important skill here, then, becomes spotting these people and either finding a way to manage them or getting away from them. You can't be politically savvy if you don't have any energy left for the really important situations. Consequently, you need to look around you and determine who is on your *list of incorrigibles*. Revisit this list now and then. People can change. Also remember that there are times when you may not have observed someone long or well enough to have taken an accurate measure. Be open to revisiting that list as circumstances change.

Fluff the Dove

"Fluffing the dove" is a conflict management strategy that interprets events in a way favorable to both parties. It gives someone who might seem to deserve a strong rebuke an opportunity to come out of the interaction looking good. To accomplish this, the person who has been offended must decide to smooth the feathers of the other party rather than retaliate. Consider, for example, the situation and possible response options below.

> **SITUATION:** *Someone has just blamed you for something that's partly her fault as well.*

> **RESPONSE OPTION 1:** *"No doubt you've found, as I have, that there is usually more to a situation than meets the eye."*

The beauty of this response is its ambiguity. You haven't said to her, "Look who's talking" or "This is as much your fault as mine," both of which clearly reciprocate blame. Instead, you've used a conversational cliché to alter the allocation of blame. If the other person replies, "Are you accusing me?" or something of this nature, you might say, "I'm simply pointing out that none of us is perfect and that digging a bit deeper often reveals a reasonable explanation. Casting blame simply cripples us in our efforts to rectify this."

> **RESPONSE OPTION 2:** *"Hindsight is often, but not always, twenty-twenty."*

Here again you haven't directly engaged her in a confrontation, especially if you've said this calmly, with no suggestion of sarcasm or attack. Your response makes the point that there are other ways to see the situation and that hers is but one of them. Were you to say, "Obviously your hindsight isn't twenty-twenty," you'd be asking for an argument. Let's say she asks you to elaborate on your response. You might then say, "We could both point fingers, but I think we'd be better off looking for a solution." This encourages her to move along if she doesn't want to get caught up in the blame Game.[4]

RESPONSE OPTION 3: *"Perhaps we would benefit from looking at this as a learning experience."*

This is another diversionary tactic. It doesn't directly reproach the person blaming you, and it doesn't place blame on you. Instead, it redefines the situation as one from which something might be gained for both parties. Once again, you need to be ready to elaborate. If she asks what you meant by your remark, you could say, "Rather than blame each other and storm out angrily, why not see if something can be learned from this unfortunate set of circumstances?" If she reacts with an angry accusation, you could say, "I'm as upset as you are about the outcome. But we'll all be better served if we spend our time seeking a solution."

RESPONSE OPTION 4: *"This project means a good deal to you and you've certainly put a great deal into it. I don't blame you a bit for how you feel right now."*

Meeting an attack with a compliment is fluffing the dove at its best. The balancing act here is that it can't be an over-the-top compliment. That would be insincere, and seen as such. Given the rule of reciprocity, your kindness should be reciprocated with at least a reduction in the intensity of the attack on you. She might reply, "You have no idea how I feel." To this you might calmly and sympathetically say, "You may be right." If she continues the attack, you might remain silent and engage in empathic listening. Look at her; nod at what she says unless it's a direct attack. When you disagree, tilt your head slightly sideways, look puzzled, then shake your head back and forth a bit to indicate that while you don't agree with her view, you still sympathize with her emotions.

RESPONSE OPTION 5: *"I'm very sorry this happened. It's very upsetting to you and, frankly, to all of us."*

Apologizing is another form of fluffing the dove. There are, however, many ways to apologize. Women do more of it than men, and—this is the critical difference—their apologies tend to take blame. When men apologize, they tend to say things like "I'm sorry this had to happen to you," rather than "I'm sorry I did it." This is because men more often have what psychologists call an "external locus of control," whereas women have an "internal locus of control." The former is a focus on external reasons for a negative situation; the latter focuses on one's personal contribution to it. This doesn't mean that women are incapable of an external orientation for blame or that men are incapable of an internal one; this just speaks to their tendencies.[5]

There are times when it's best to use the "I'm sorry that happened" (external locus of control) approach. It sounds like an apology, but it's more of an expression of sympathy. If you say, "I'm very sorry," you accept blame even if you don't mean to do so. Save that for situations when you are personally sorry. By being sorry the outcome occurred, you placate the person blaming you to some extent by including the word "sorry," but you don't place yourself at the center of the blame target. By adding that everyone present is also upset, you suggest that the issue isn't just about her. You've all suffered. This approach limits her options, to some extent, by enlarging the target. You've placed yourself in a larger camp. And you've changed the subject from blame to one of shared distress. You've done so without attacking her, so according to the rule of reciprocity, she is somewhat obliged to return the favor.

Notice that in all these options the main idea is to keep calm, rise above personal vindictiveness, take the high road, and whenever possible make the other person feel good about herself, all of which will help you feel good about yourself.

Managing Upward Conflict

I've worked privately with many CEOs and senior executives to manage conflicts with those at higher levels. Usually, they've found themselves in a "personality clash" with someone in a position to determine their fate. As you can imagine, this can be a real career stopper.

There is definitely an art to managing upward conflict. Most people walk around living a lie, disguising their true feelings about their bosses. Much of this is very functional. If we all said whatever we felt whenever we felt like it, there could be no organizations. The very term "organization" implies that people are getting along to achieve common goals, and most of us keep a good many thoughts to ourselves in order to get through the day or to advance our careers.

While this is often a functional coping strategy, it becomes destructive when the organization or individuals in it begin to suffer. This happens a lot in the pathological arenas described in chapter 2. For example, people who don't like the boss will engage in what have been labeled "carnival techniques,"[6] when employees stage festive gatherings in which the boss is demonized and ridiculed. In other cases, subordinates become "moles" for a disliked boss. They pretend to dislike the boss and engage in what was described earlier as "apparent self-disclosure"—appearing to reveal private thoughts about the boss so others will be inclined to reciprocate with theirs. In this way they get people to say negative things about the boss which they then pass on to him in the hope of currying favor. Another common tactic is to do "the dirty work" for the boss to prove loyalty and thereby get ahead. Many choose this role as a survival technique, and some even come to enjoy it. Those people are really dangerous.

How do you protect yourself in such environments? One way is to get out, and fast. If that is not an option, some people decide to fight fire with fire. They outmaneuver the maneuverers. One way is to get to the boss first with things—keep him or her in the loop. Another is to use inoculation, described earlier, casually dropping information about possible well-poisoning so that when it does occur, the boss is inclined to be skeptical or dismiss it. Another alternative, which I call the "bob-and-weave strategy," is avoiding involvement in teams and discussions that bring you in contact with people you know to be destructively deceptive.

Sometimes you have to simply stand up for yourself. One CEO that I worked with—I'll call him Fred—was having difficulty with his board of directors. Their high regard for the prior CEO was making it difficult for Fred to gain acceptance. After Fred and I worked together to get the lay of the land in terms of board member personalities and priorities and after I'd talked with one of Fred's trusted direct reports, we strategized for the upcoming board meeting.

Fred's leadership style was Supportive. The prior CEO had a Commanding style. Before the meeting, we took the points Fred wanted to make and developed them to suit the styles of the board members. Particular attention was given to those board members known to be antagonistic. Questions were generated to assess rather than assume where they stood on issues. Using a role-play format, we worked on Fred's delivery style to create an impression of being in charge without overdoing it. The results were outstanding.

Fortunately, Fred sees the board members only occasionally, so he doesn't have to step out of his comfortable Supportive style often. And even with them, he doesn't have to relinquish it entirely. He now has the ability, though, to stretch when he needs to, and this has garnered him considerable respect from those previously dubious of his potential.

There are no perfect bosses or boards because there are no perfect people. But if you find yourself having to engage in too many uncomfortable tactics just to get through each day, you're not headed for the secret handshake. The best bet is probably making a clean cut. Get into a division or organization where you and the boss see eye-to-eye.

The Obvious Difference—Gender

The impressions people form of each other and of what others have said complicate conflict resolution because many of those impressions are difficult to access due to socialization processes. For example, men and women experience life, and therefore work as well, in different ways. The way they communicate these experiences is often also different. As Carol Gilligan points out in her book *A Different Voice*, since it is difficult to say "different" without saying "better" or "worse," when women's behaviors don't conform to those adhered to by men, and vice versa, each gender group tends to conclude that something is wrong with the other.[7] True players have the skill to recognize this trap, realize it can limit their options, and are careful to avoid letting it do so.

The Thin Pink Line

During my interview with Carol Kovac, vice president of Life Sciences Solutions at IBM, the term "thin pink line" entered our conversation. We had been talking about the narrow parameters within which women's actions at work are interpreted. The movie *The Thin Red Line* had just been released. It offered a useful descriptor of the difficult line women perceive themselves walking when they're in male-dominated organizations. At Carol's suggestion, we simply changed "red" to "pink."

Research indicates that how women dress, walk, and talk within a work environment has a great likelihood of being noticed because women are usually the minority. In order not to attract negative attention and make men focus more on their femininity than on what they're saying, women often walk a thin line. Step outside of this line and career-stalling derogatory labels are likely to be assigned to women.

As I see it, people are going to label you anyway, so you might as well have some input. One of the obstacles for women trying to achieve the secret handshake is believing that they're better off keeping a low profile and not being labeled a "troublemaker." In reality, the only trouble here is the one caused by keeping on the sidelines rather than taking some calculated risks.

Kovac says that while both men and women need to be competent to be promoted, there's a greater tendency to promote men on potential and women on their track record. So you have to let people know what you've done. Kovac believes, "You can't wait for someone to notice you, worry that you're bothering the boss with your accomplishments, or neglect to let someone know that you really want to work with him." Kovac recommends that people link what they've done to the criteria used by their companies to assess promotion potential. This is good advice no matter where you work. You need to know what criteria matter, connect what you do to those, and, as Kovac says, don't expect other people to do it for you.

Women need to stop worrying about being labeled as too feminine or too unfeminine, and get on with getting noticed and appreciated. Kathleen Brown, president of Bank of America Private Bank West, thinks women in their fifties are a real find for companies. They've learned the ropes and are willing to go after what they want. As long as they're doing the other politically sophisticated things we've discussed, being a bit "feminine" now and then isn't a career breaker for these women. In fact, it can be quite the opposite.

When Carly Fiorina was promoted to CEO of Hewlett-Packard in 1999, the press sought to find out how she did it. Here was a medieval history major who had taught English in Italy and hadn't joined AT&T until she was twenty-five. Nevertheless, at age forty-four she was selected to run one of the world's computer giants. Why? Her rise has been attributed not only to her exceptional competence but to her inspirational team style. She sent flowers and gifts to workers to thank them and often left grateful messages on their voice mail at night. She is viewed by tech industry observers as both "energetic and adaptable," capable of conjoining sensitivity and determination.[8]

Research indicates that women tend to be giving. Take the

favor bank, for instance. For many women, it's unfeminine to want something in return. That's why women make themselves available for jobs that a lot of men wouldn't touch. Men do favors, but most know and accept that there will come a time when a favor will be expected in return. One of my male colleagues got something for just about everything he did. Borrow a pencil from him and he'd ask for a favor. While he was to my way of thinking a bit too direct about his quid pro quos, at least he knew the value of not giving away resources without getting something in return. Many women want to please and to be liked, so they do things for these reasons alone. What they don't see is that their work time is worth much more. Someone who wants it should be willing to give something in return. This is especially the case when someone is asking for a significant amount of time or is taking you away from a project that needs to be completed soon. Unfortunately, however, a typical scenario between male and female coworkers looks like this:

BILL: Marie, could you fill in for me at the meeting tomorrow?

MARIE: I've got a lot going on tomorrow, Bill.

BILL: If I don't show, it'll be noticed, but I can't get out of the other meeting.

MARIE: Okay, Bill. I'll do it.

BILL: Great. Thanks.

Marie is reluctantly doing a favor for Bill. She has not, however, signaled to him that there is a cost to him. She may think that he will pay her back sometime down the road, but if Bill is used to taking and not reciprocating, Marie may be giving up her valuable time and getting nothing in return.

In my observations of male favor-swapping, signals are sent either subtly or directly to let the borrower know that something valuable has been given and that the human rule of reciprocity will someday, if not today, kick in. Women are often loath to be other than altruistic.

So how should a woman send the message that her time is valuable and that she expects some return? That depends on her style. If she's direct, she might take this approach:

BILL: Marie, could you fill in for me at the meeting tomorrow?

MARIE: I've got a lot going on tomorrow, Bill.

BILL: If I don't show, it'll be noticed, but I can't get out of the other meeting.

MARIE: Okay, Bill. I'll do it this time. But you owe me one.

BILL: You got it.

If Marie knows that Bill is the type to forget what he owes, she might be better off asking for something on the spot. For example, she might say, "Okay, Bill. But I'll need two hours of your time on Friday morning between ten and noon to help me get a project completed on time."

The Self-Promotion Trap

People judge behaviors by comparing them to what others in similar circumstances are doing. This is called "social comparison."[9] If, for example, there is a new male boss to whom all the men are introducing themselves and the woman is not, the male boss is likely to compare her unfavorably with the others who seem to know the unstated rule: Get to the new boss before he gets rid of you.

Now, it is possible for a sophisticated male boss or peer to realize that a female colleague might be operating by a different set of rules. He might be misinterpreting her desire to let him get adjusted before she bothers him as an unwillingness to be part of the team or even as a dislike for him. This second interpretation is even more likely if it's known that she got along well with the prior boss. It wouldn't be unusual for the new male boss to assume that this woman who keeps a distance is doing so because she is not happy about his arrival.

Let's turn this situation around. While research shows that women are less inclined than men to self-promote, a female boss could find annoying a man's efforts to be front-and-center.[10] In fact, many women executives have complained to me about what they call "male posturing." They see it as a throwback to another era, a kind of bravado that seems to them more surface than substance. So what's a male aspiring subordinate to do in such cases? Does he engage in the "posturing" he sees around him from other men, or does he tailor or temper it to his immediate female boss?

This is where political savvy comes in. As they say, when in Rome do as the Romans do. If your boss doesn't overtly self-promote, you shouldn't either. Now and then people resist this rule of thumb. They argue that they shouldn't have to adapt to a boss who "doesn't get it," whether male or female. That's where the true player would disagree. He or she knows that adaptability is important—that men and women are different and expecting your boss to do all the work of getting past gender differences is setting yourself up for disappointment. The crucial point here is that you can let such differences get in the way, or you can decide that you're going to minimize their potential downside effects by meeting the other person halfway. That's what the women and men who've reached the top have done.

Never Limit Your Mentors to People Who Look Like You

Whether obvious differences are gender-related or cultural, it's easy to fall into the trap of thinking that people not like you are unlikely to be of help. This is a limiting perspective and one that's in large part false. Ask anyone who has gotten the secret handshake and they'll tell you that people who helped them along the way were quite different from themselves. The people most like you may see you as competition. The person who is surprised that you asked for his or her help may be flattered. If so, he or she is likely to be of assistance.

Nearly all the people I interviewed for this book told me about someone unlike themselves who helped them get ahead. Carly Fiorina became CEO of Hewlett-Packard by making some very powerful allies of men. She realized, as the politically savvy do, that sticking solely with people who are like yourself isn't going to get you the gold ring; getting a helping hand to the secret handshake is often in good part a matter of having the ability to see past surface differences.

Some people are so busy getting themselves ahead or keeping themselves there that they aren't worth approaching even if they could pass for your twin. There are a lot of other people out there, however, who'd be glad to help if someone unlike themselves would ask. And if there might be something in it for them, they'd be all the more inclined.

A Few Final Thoughts
on Conflict

Negotiation research has consistently demonstrated that conflict is important in reaching optimal solutions. But there is considerable complexity involved in making conflict a good thing. A common assumption by experts is that if conflict focuses on tasks, not on people, the outcome is more likely to be positive. But attacking people's work is often synonymous with attacking them, especially if done in insensitive ways.

Rather than make sweeping statements about how conflict is good, it's better to consider it good if it's handled in a professional manner: that is, engaging in enlightened self-interest without damaging the other party in any public fashion.

In some parts of the world, public attacks are part of looking committed to your goals. In others, they're a sure sign of losing control and being a cad. Organizational interpretations vary as well. You need to know what type of organization you're in to know the best ways to handle conflict. Some people make large career jumps by standing up to authority and making their ideas clear, when others were too afraid to do so.

It's a matter again of reading the tea leaves—knowing when to make a stand and even risk insulting someone because the goal is important. Even in such circumstances, though, at some point in the conflict there will be an opening when settlement is possible, when angst turns to anticipation of a solution. The politically savvy know when this is. The best of them always have one ear to the door of resolution, and when the time seems right, they open it.

12.

Cultivating Influence

———■———

I recently met for dinner with one of the most influential attorneys in
the United States. Selected by presidents and business leaders as their
attorney of choice, he naturally has some thoughts about influence:

*You really can't learn when you're talking. So I listen. I ask the
people to reenact what is bothering them. I watch their nonverbal
communication—how they sit, whether their arms are folded, if
they're glaring or rolling their eyes. You have to read the room
quickly. The point is to listen intently to find out who wants what.
Everyone gets to tell you why their solution is the best. My job is
to create some ease in the room. Then, after a while, you begin to
hear overlaps in their solutions. And once you convince them there
are no solutions without compromise, you work with them to discover a solution that brings together some part of each person's interests.*

Persuasion is more often an activity of aligning previously disparate ideas than convincing passive others to set aside their views to accept someone else's. The talent is in the ability to listen and learn where the *links* are among the views being presented. The reason why so many people can't find these important links is that they're too busy thinking about their response, what they consider to be the very best possible rebuttal. In doing so, they fail to realize that persuasion works better and longer if all parties walk away feeling that some part of what they cared about was considered or granted.

So what does this mean in terms of the politics of work? It means that you should try to find in what people say ideas that easily connect to yours. In chapter 9 we looked at this in terms of power. Now we'll apply it to persuasion in general. Assume that you want to be assigned to an important project. The natural tendency is to go into the boss's office and begin rattling off all of the reasons why you should get that assignment. This isn't the best way. Instead, you should begin with questions, such as "What are you hoping will come out of the new project?" or "I've heard a lot of rumors about the new project, but I don't really think I know its primary purpose. Can you tell me?" From there, listen for openings in the boss's reply that allow you to connect your aspirations with her description. Let's assume she says, "I want this group to come up with a marketing plan that the competition can't touch. It's a lot to ask, and they're feeling the pressure. But they'll get past it, I'm sure, and then they'll start cooking with some great ideas." At this point, if one of your talents is facilitation, you might say, "I'd be glad to help out, after hours if necessary, in the role of a facilitator. As you know, that was my role on the last project, and it got us off to an earlier start than we might have if we hadn't ironed out our differences at the outset and calmed some of the team members' fears."

By taking this approach, you connect your skills—what you have to offer—with what she needs. By offering to help even beyond normal work hours, you demonstrate your commitment and strong desire to be involved, without seeming desperate. If you merely give her all the reasons why she should choose you and none of them match what she really cares about, the likelihood of being persuasive is very low.

The ACE Model

Through my years studying persuasion and consulting on the topic, I've developed a tool for selecting the strongest logic. It's called "THE ACE Model." Based on decades of persuasion research, this model categorizes persuasive appeals into three primary types: appropriateness, consistency, and effectiveness.

Appeals to *appropriateness* use the opinions or actions of others to encourage a person to do what you'd like him or her to do. For example, if you'd like someone who works for you to accept a transfer, you might point out, "Everyone who's been promoted to senior management has done this" or "Lots of people take transfers they don't want out of loyalty." Mentioning that others do something often encourages people to do it too.

Consistency appeals are those in which the persuader tells the other party that what he might do is somehow consistent with his personality, likes, or dislikes. With regard to a transfer, a consistency appeal might sound like this: "It isn't like you to miss such a great opportunity" or "You're so adventurous. I was sure you'd jump at a chance like this."

Effectiveness appeals suggest that an action is going to bring desired outcomes. In the case of the transfer, you might point out,

"If you take this transfer now, they'll likely bring you back as a vice-president" or "Going to Atlanta has always been the way this company grooms its best candidates for senior management." Of course, these claims must be anchored in fact.

Being savvy in the skills of persuasion means understanding which type of appeal fits the situation at hand. You have to listen to people's likes and dislikes, whether they care about the opinions of others or consider themselves to be guided by their individual tastes and interests. If you select an appeal to appropriateness when the person really cares about doing something that makes him feel independent and unique, your efforts will likely fail.

Edward Reardon, senior technical fellow and director, Advanced Materials, at Shipley Company LLC, remembers earlier in his career convincing his colleagues to salvage a new product that hadn't performed as well as hoped in pre-launch tests. "It happens more often than not in the development of new products," Reardon told me. "So you have to wrest success out of failure. In this case, the product was cheap and that's partly why we developed it. Just before we were ready to scrap the whole thing, I reminded everyone that the product had a very important characteristic, one we'd focused on for good reasons: It *was* cheap. That's what our customers were demanding. So maybe they'd take a slightly less desirable product if it were to sell for sufficiently less money than the competitors' superior ones. We could then work on perfecting it. So we went to the marketing guys, sold the idea to them, and they sold it to the customer. It was a case of snatching victory from defeat all because we knew what the customer was looking for and were able to focus on that."

Obviously, this kind of approach wouldn't be successful if the customer wanted the highest quality. But often people prefer "good enough" products over expensive ones. Cubic zirconia would be worthless if people always had to have diamonds. But if what a customer cares about is shininess and low price, then there's room in the jewelry market for something less rare and precious than diamonds. The cubic zirconia customer is interested in financial effectiveness.

Finding out whether people care more about being appropriate, consistent, or effective is critical to effective persuasion. The most persuasive argument is invariably the one that addresses the primary interests of the person you wish to persuade.

Frame Your Position in an Attractive Way

Framing, as described earlier, is a crucial influence tactic. Picture two people having a disagreement. The events can be framed as a *fight* or as a *debate of the issues*. The latter is less personal and destructive. If you are advocating the hiring of a particular candidate, you don't want to tell your boss that during the interview process the candidate seemed "stubborn." It would create a negative impression. Instead, you could describe her as "persistent." Then the chances of her being hired would be significantly increased. The same set of behaviors can be described, or framed, in very different ways. Influential people know how to frame to their advantage.

From this example alone it's easy to see how wonderful a skill framing is. As mentioned earlier, we operate daily more on inference and judgment than on fact. We see a man standing next to a fallen potted plant and we assume that he knocked it over. Sometimes we even imagine that we actually saw him do it. If we see a child throw a ball in the direction of another child who suddenly starts crying, we might assume that the child who threw the ball is inconsiderate or unkind. If we knew the whole story, we might come to quite a different conclusion.

To be politically adept, then, it's important to think before speaking to edit out words and phrases that do not advance your position. I remember listening to a CEO speak to a conference gathering of primarily women. He said with great pride, "I am very encouraging of women working. If my wife wanted to work, I'd let her."

If you look at that last sentence, the phrase "I'd let her" suggests that he would be the one making the ultimate decision, which contradicts his attempt to demonstrate his open-minded views. Even a few ill-chosen words can undermine credibility.

Think Gray

It's important to teach yourself to *think gray* when other people are seeing black and white. This is one of the hallmarks of a person on his or her way to the top.

The rule here is: Don't respond to people in terms of right or wrong, true or false, black or white, or other polarities, but rather in terms of shades of gray. Invite complexity so long as you don't allow it to cloud judgment. A Fortune 500 board chairman told me that he even creates a kind of fog in situations where people on each side of an issue are both convinced that they're right. "I generate confusion by asking questions, leading them to consider perspectives and options that hadn't crossed their minds. Then when they are sufficiently unsure of the veracity of their claims, I bring them gradually back to a conclusion that borrows from both of the original views while incorporating some of the fog."

Contrary to popular opinion, the best managers do far less

telling than they do asking. And why are they so inquisitive? They know that the best answers emerge from unearthing the complexities of people and situations. "Gray thinkers" aren't inhibited by policies. They're the first to question them or to propose that the situation at hand might be an exception to the rule. Consequently, their worlds are not a neat series of do's and don'ts, but rather avenues of extensive possibilities.

Be Concise, Clear, on Track, and Watch the Subtle Cues

Time is of the essence at work. Yet most managers clutter their discussions and arguments with tangential information: Their meetings are too long, their directions convoluted. Being concise, to the point, and clear are indispensable to good management.

Of course, if this were easy to do, everyone would be doing it. Self-discipline is the key. You need to listen to yourself and watch how people respond. If they're looking distracted, it's time to get to the point in a persuasive, perhaps emphatic way. To that end, there are a number of words, called "emphasis words," that spice up otherwise boring comments. If everything you say is conveyed in the same tone with little use of words indicating which points are most important, people tune out. If you listen carefully to people who are successful, you hear words like "critical," "fundamental," "imperative," and "absolute" peppering their speeches. You'll also hear such phrases as "If you only take away one thing from this discussion today, make it . . ." or "The essential part of what we've said so far is . . ."

Aside from emphasis, truly articulate people stay on track in conversations. When they do digress from the main topic, they return to it and show how the digression is related. Communication scholars call this "conversational coherence." When two people pay close attention to each other's speech and connect their comments to those of the other, they are both engaged in coherence. Unfortunately, many conversations are more like sequential speeches in which each person pays little attention to what the other just said. This isn't persuasive. It suggests that you haven't been listening or that you don't care. You don't see politically savvy people ignoring coherence. If they need to change topics, they do so skillfully by finding a way to gracefully connect what was said to the new topic.

There is considerable detail to be considered in communicating in an effective, persuasive way. There are rules at every turn which we, as people who've communicated for years, no longer feel we need to think about. For example, when someone talks, it is the obligation of the other party or parties to provide some supportive rituals in the form of nods or utterances that indicate they've accepted his right to speak. They may disagree with what he says or even dismiss it, but they must look at him as he speaks and provide some evidence of at least passing interest if they wish to avoid overt rudeness.

Since we all know this rule, it's possible to use it to send messages of rebuff. I recently saw a vice-president do this to one of his reports, by listening and even nodding but providing terse verbal replies and less than full eye contact. In this way, the VP was able to fulfill his politeness obligation with the nods, but by limiting eye contact and verbally responding with unusual brevity he let the subordinate know that he was displeased. It was a mini-rebuff. A full-fledged rebuff probably wouldn't have included the nods. The subordinate picked up on the message and eased his way out of the conversation to join another one across the room.

This subordinate later confided in me that his superior prides himself on being "supportive" but that as you get to know him you find that he isn't. He dismisses people subtly so that he can deny having done so. His array of conversational rituals tells people when they're welcome to continue speaking, and when they should speed up, slow down, or go away. Subordinates who don't learn to read these cues end up finding other jobs. The politically astute, however, see the contradictions in the messages and act upon them in ways that preserve their jobs and, if they are sufficiently artful, even bring them positive regard.

How to manage conversations persuasively is a book in itself. The most important rule is to listen to yourself and watch what is going on around you. No idea is so important that it doesn't need a good introduction, sensitivity to ritual to get it to the floor, supportive data, and credit given to those hearing it. No idea should be dragged out longer than need be, and whenever possible it should be connected clearly to the interests of the listeners.

Allow Yourself to Be Gracefully Wrong

There are few things so disarming as an apology when defensiveness is expected. The idea that you must have all the answers in order to win respect is false. Research shows that in anything other than life-and-death situations, people prefer to follow the fallible person over the supposedly infallible one. Respect does come to those who earn it, but they don't earn it by always being right. It comes more often to those who, at least on occasion, know how to be gracefully wrong.

The point here is not to go around apologizing regularly. But if you are wrong, acknowledge it. As discussed in chapter 11, one reason we avoid apologies is that they seem to make us appear weak. Yet an apology that isn't accompanied by exaggerated self-deprecation can be very powerful, very persuasive. It can bring people who were opposed to you over to your side.

Tim Romer, chief financial officer of Adexa software developers, sees this ability to keep relations positive especially important in small organizations. "In small companies there's a large need for consensus. You can't bypass people with whom you're in opposition. You see them every day. In large organizations maneuvering is subtle and there are a lot of different levels and ways to get things done. There's more sibling rivalry in smaller organizations, more intense complaining, and fewer options." If you want to work effectively in this kind of environment, Romer says, "You have to put petty self-interests aside to advance the team or company goals."

It takes a strong person to put petty interests aside or to admit he or she is wrong, especially after the fact. Phrases such as "I wasn't thinking that time," "Where was my brain on that one?" or "This isn't my finest moment" can be useful. They're brief and not overly self-deflating. Of course, there are times when a sincere apology of greater length may be necessary. Most of the time, though, short and sweet and definitely sincere is a good rule of thumb.

Chris Argyris, management expert, published an article in the *Harvard Business Review* about communication that blocks learning. He described the extensive efforts we put into making things go our way. "All of us design our behavior in order to remain in unilateral control, to maximize winning and minimize losing." The reason for this strategy is "to avoid vulnerability, risk, embarrassment, and the appearance of incompetence."[1] As reasonable as this goal appears, it is not only deeply defensive but also a recipe for what Argyris calls "antilearning."

The scariest result of such self-protective, avoid-vulnerability-at-all-cost strategies is that we don't get a chance to reflect on our actions, to do better next time. Most important, we don't allow ourselves to be wrong in front of others. Research tells us that people prefer to be with and even work for somewhat fallible people, probably because the pressure to be perfect in their eyes isn't so great.[2]

Argyris rightly argues that we are adrift in defensive routines at work. Yet, politically sophisticated people know when they are engaging in routines that keep them from truly reflecting on their behavior. And, just as important, they also see through organizational defensive routines that exist to keep the organization from self-reflection, such as when people in high-level positions create rules and practices that discourage challenges. This routine reflects a keep-them-in-the-dark approach to management. It is difficult, however, to keep politically astute people in the dark for long. Like the advantage that accrues to those who carry lanterns in the dark, the politically sophisticated see not only rules and practices but also whom those rules and practices serve.

One way to protect yourself from being kept in the dark is to find allies in high places. This works particularly well in organizations where it's acceptable to go around the boss if there's a good reason for doing so. Find a truly fair-minded person, preferably one who's been through this himself or who despises political roadblocks to progress. Make him an ally. Be sure his opinion is valued more in the organization than that of the person blocking your path.

Patricia Michaels, successful sales executive for one of the largest high-tech companies in the United States, is not averse to going around her boss. "I'm in the process of strategizing a couple of objectives that I know my direct boss will not endorse," she told me. "I am not even going to present them to her directly. Instead, I will present an eighteen-month plan to her boss and get agreement on the vision. I have a good relationship with him and he will view it as mentoring. I'll be very clear about asking for his support in taking this to the next step, and I'll ask if he minds if I touch base with him as I need more advice. This will give me his buy-in. Then I'll work out the tactics with my direct boss."

By presenting her ideas within the context of an eighteen-month plan that needed a look-see by a high-level person whose mentoring expertise could help shape it, Michaels found a means of getting her ideas past a roadblock boss to someone who can make things happen. She can't do this too often, and in some cultures it's political suicide. But by packaging it in the way she did, it looks less like bypassing a boss than it does seeking mentoring.

Many people don't want to do these things. They think "making waves" will ruin their careers. That's another myth used to keep people from challenging the system. Supposedly, the word will get out and you'll be blacklisted for life. The truth is that it takes more than standing up for yourself to be blacklisted. And some blacklists are a badge of honor. On the positive side, if you go about gaining allies without causing the people blocking you too much loss of face, you may get what you want and find a way to mend fences later. The best allies know how to help you make this happen.

Choose the Right Communication Channel

Michael Eisner considers e-mail so dangerous to companies and careers that he made it the topic of his 2000 keynote graduation speech at the University of Southern California. The primary reason for most of the conflicts at Disney, Eisner told the graduates, their relatives and friends, and the faculty, is technology-based. "The intensity within our company is higher than ever and I'm convinced it's because of e-mail." Eisner considers most of us "frighteningly unprepared" for modern communication technologies like e-mail. As he explained, it takes years to learn that there are different ways to talk with different people and to know when to pause before pushing the send button. Eisner considers this tendency a candidate among dangers that can bring down a company. "If you say, 'You dope,' over dinner, it can be endearing, but with e-mail it can be shocking." He described how an e-mail discussion between two of his executives became heated when one of them wrote a sarcastic comment that might have passed as a joke in face-to-face conversation. Eisner read the e-mail and acknowledged that the comment in question had "hit a nerve," but largely because the communication channel, void of the subtle messages of face-to-face, had "amplified the sarcasm." Spell-check doesn't check for anger and sarcasm.[3]

As companies turn increasingly to on-line teamwork, the issue of when to use which channel of communication will become more important and complex. Net teams collaborating via the Internet from geographically dispersed locations are already finding that access to knowledge repositories allowing entries to be made by any team member at any time often creates too much information. Those people whose contributions to such repositories are too long or short, too disorganized, or too hasty find themselves unappreciated by team members thousands of miles away.

Ann Majchrzak, specialist in design and management of technology change, found this to be the case at Rocketdyne in the company's efforts to substantially cut the cost of rocket engines. The team assigned to this project used a collaborative tool, "The Internet Notebook," that allowed members of the virtual team to remotely access the ideas, observations, and opinions of other team members. Majchrzak noted that the team originally decided to enter and share all information using this technology but soon found that too much information was being generated and that much of it had only transient utility or, because so many ideas were generated, was quickly obsolete.[4]

The ability to use Internet notebooks of this sort in an effective manner requires cyberspace political savvy. Knowing what information is of potential interest and what is boring or obsolete, knowing how to engage people in dialogue so that the best solutions emerge, and recognizing that what you send is permanently recorded for all to see are important considerations in this era of quick information access.

Whether you're using e-mail or a new form of communication technology, it's wise to consider how the characteristics of that channel might impact the extent and nature of your influence. Choosing wisely among channel options requires sensitivity to potential misreading. Rule number one is: If the issue is delicate, don't fire off your ideas. The send and reply buttons are not friends in such circumstances. From a receiver vantage point, don't assume that you have received an e-mail in the spirit in which it was sent if your interpretation is negative. Give the sender a technology benefit of the doubt. Call or go see him or her to check perceptions.

Some companies communicate by e-mail even if the recipient is in the next-door office. They do so for the purpose of efficiency. And they end up doing so in the service of misconception. Employees in such organizations have the dubious honor of belonging to one senior executive I interviewed calls "the elite e-mail level." They get hundreds of e-mails a day. It's a club you don't want to join.

The second rule for choosing a communication channel: Know your channel strength and that of the person with whom you'll be communicating. Some people are terrible on the telephone. If you or the person you're calling is one of them, don't handle an important issue this way. If your boss or someone who can help you achieve the secret handshake isn't a phone person, meet him or her face-to-face. Use e-mail for conveying information not likely to be misconstrued. In all cases, choose the persuasion channel that suits the message and the people. If you are a terrible speller too rushed to spell-check, don't use e-mail when communicating with people in a position to make or break your career.

While these two rules might seem to be common sense, they are not commonly applied. Technology has provided easy, quick access, and, in so doing, has provided opportunities for easy, quick interpersonal problems at work. Technology is a tool and like all tools is suited to certain purposes. Right now most of us are so enamored with what we can do with new technologies that we neglect to consider whether we should.

Manage the Number of Issues

Whenever possible, handle one primary issue at a time whether you're talking on the telephone, faxing, e-mailing, or even speaking face-to-face. I recently worked with two senior executives of a highly profitable interior design company who were squabbling. They had similar goals and even generally liked each other, but their communication was always cluttered. On the first day we met, one of them handed me a memo he'd written to the other. He was proud of the memo because it laid out in what he thought to be a clear manner how he felt about a number of the two managers' differences. Pleased with its clarity, he failed to notice its complexity. It included five things on which he disagreed with the other manager. Even though his memo had started out with a friendly tone indicating that the information to follow was being sent in a spirit of cooperation rather than criticism, the rest of the memo contradicted this. While it was indeed clear, it was insulting. No one wants to read five things he's doing wrong. What do people focus on if they get such a memo? They focus on how much they dislike the sender.

If it's important enough to put in a memo, it's important enough to get its own memo. If it borders on insult or might be construed as such, and that is not the sender's intention, then the information doesn't belong in a memo in the first place.

The main point of this chapter is that influence is critical to achieving the secret handshake. The second point is that mastering influence is a matter of knowing how to position ideas effectively, how to time the delivery of those ideas, and how to select the right communication channel. The inner circles of most companies consist of people who have learned to make these judgments.

13.

Politically Astute Negotiating

———■———

No one gets to the top without skillful negotiation. When told something can't be done, truly effective negotiators think about how they *can* get it done. When told they *must* do something, they begin to think of how they might do it to their advantage, or not do it at all. Telling them "no" or "this is not negotiable" is equivalent to issuing them a challenge. Their brains shift into a negotiation gear at the merest hint of being blocked.

I've spent a good part of my career studying what separates those who get a good deal from those who settle prematurely or don't bother to negotiate at all. Insights gleaned from that study, in addition to the experiences of dozens of people I've interviewed, form the core of this chapter. It takes considerable study and practice to become an expert negotiator, and some very good books have been published on the subject. But what it takes to be a politically astute or street-smart negotiator is somewhat different. That's our focus here.

Preparing for Street-Smart Negotiation

"When I'm negotiating an important deal," a New York City–based negotiation expert with an impressive clientele told me, "I listen for quite a while. As I present a proposal, I watch to see if several people seem opposed to it. In that case, I do a little constructive deception. If one of them expresses some agreement with me, I might use him to divide the group. After coaxing him to my side, I'll gradually turn against him myself. The others, who are by then angry with him, become more open to my proposal, especially if I throw in some things they want. Essentially, the person who initially agreed with me becomes the common enemy. And nothing brings people together so well as that."

This is hardball negotiation. In fact, in this type of scenario most people don't even see the ball coming. It's a counterintuitive strategy because negotiators usually try to locate someone who agrees with them, then look for a way to create a win-win outcome. Instead, the above negotiation expert engages in "constructive deception," outwitting a cohesive group by locating its most cooperative member and alienating him.

This example alone shows how important it is to develop street-smart negotiation skills. You have to distrust the obvious, and recognize hardball tactics when you see them.

Impression Traps

Faulty impressions are the number one enemy of negotiation effectiveness, especially in politicized organizations. "They'll never fire us" are the famous last words of many people who find themselves invited to leave organizations. It's always better to enter any situation with healthy skepticism about your assumptions and some acquired insights into what the assumptions are of the other negotiators.

Consider the assumptions of the following three people about to enter into an important business negotiation. They've come together to negotiate a product production and distribution deal between two companies: Customware (Mike and Ellen's company) and Blueprint (Gene's company). The deal could strengthen Blueprint's presence in Europe and give Customware an entrée into the European market. Having met briefly earlier in the evening, they're in their hotel rooms preparing for the next day's negotiation. Here are their thoughts:

Gene had Mike figured. He'd seen the type before—aloof, arrogant even—the kind that looks right through you, doesn't give an inch until you've given away the farm, and then makes you think he's done you a favor. The thing to do was wait him out, feign indifference, stare him down if necessary, and make him sweat. Treat any gesture of accommodation with skepticism. Gene prided himself on being able to tell a tiger by its stripes. This one didn't know who he was dealing with.

The woman, thought Gene, was more difficult to read. She had depth—you could see that in her eyes. But what difference did it make? Ellen is just along for the experience. Maybe they planned to play "good cop, bad cop" with him. For their own sake, Gene thought, they'd better have a backup plan.

Reading his own bio on the plane had bolstered Mike's confidence, not that much bolstering was necessary. His M.B.A. said all that needed to be said. Gene didn't have one. It wasn't snob-bery, Mike assured himself. He had met some crafty negotiators in his time who hadn't had fancy degrees, but Gene didn't strike him as particularly savvy. This observation, coupled with his own superior intellect, was enough to make Mike feel pretty sure of who'd walk away with the best deal. Their brief meeting ear-lier in the evening had only confirmed these impressions.

Mike's biggest challenge was on his own team. Why had his boss sent Ellen? Sure she was smart—had an M.B.A. and her record in sales and marketing had made him her equal in status. But this would be a crucial negotiation. Her credentials would do her little good when the heat was on. Hopefully, she would fol-low his lead, maintain a low profile, and keep her input to a minimum. He'd tell her his expectations in the morning. The most important thing was the negotiation's outcome, not whose ego got stroked. It was time to stop thinking. He'd need his rest after such a long trip—even to take on a lightweight thinker like Gene.

Before turning off the lights in strange hotel rooms, Ellen always arranged her clothes and her ideas for the next day, made a few notes about people to call, and eased herself into sleep with a novel. Tonight, though, she couldn't get her mind off the few minutes she'd spent earlier in the evening with Gene and Mike. The body language of the two men had told her neither of them saw her as a player—even Mike, who was on her team. This was nothing new to her—part of the territory as the younger partner and a woman to boot. She'd have to set Mike straight early on. She was confident, having learned from some well-placed snitches at the home office that he'd lost some ground of late.

People weren't impressed any longer with such hard chargers,
especially in international circles where this project could take
them. The John Wayne days were ending, but Mike was obvi-
ously stuck in a style rut. He was the take-control, take-no-
prisoners type. As she dozed off, she practiced how she'd manage
Mike the next day. She didn't come thousands of miles just to
cheer him on.

Gene, Mike, and Ellen are three people on the path to negotiation failure. Gene believes he has Mike figured out because he's seen
his type before. He decides he won't be fooled this time. There's no
indication that he intends to check any of his assumptions or seek
more details. Why bother? He read a few road signs and decided he
has all the facts he needs.

Mike is no different in this regard. He has himself convinced
that his M.B.A. is the ticket to success with the supposedly less
accomplished Gene. He has already decided that Ellen is a liability despite her track record. Ellen has concluded that both Gene
and Mike have excluded any possibility that she might be important to this negotiation. She decides to make setting them
straight her first priority. In only a few minutes' time, each of
these people has charted a course for the next day—the wrong
course.

In most negotiations, instincts overtake reason. When negotiating, our mouths can start running before our minds have a
chance to filter. We react and we blow the deal before it's even off
the ground. Truly effective negotiators monitor their reactions
and think ahead to how their choice of responses might shape
those of the other person. They avoid the tendency to react with-

out checking assumptions and confirming the other person's meanings.

Most important, effective negotiators prioritize well. They steer around issues that might take them down a path away from important goals. They bypass or minimize small annoyances and occasional petty comments to assure their primary goals will be attained.

Let's take Gene as a case in point. He is about to approach Mike with a wait-him-out, feign-indifference, stare-him-down-if-necessary, and make-him-sweat series of strategies. He'll treat any gesture of accommodation with skepticism.

There's nothing wrong with Gene formulating a first impression, but that's all it is—a *first* impression. It's like the first draft of a paper. Rely on it and you *blow the deal.* Do you hand it in just because you've written a hundred papers before, or do you reread, revise, and spell-check it? Gene is about to hand in his first draft, a terrible error in judgment.

Are You the Right Person to Negotiate?

There's the possibility that Gene, Mike, and Ellen aren't the best threesome to negotiate this deal. The likelihood of them recognizing this is low, given their focus on personalities more than on the deal itself. That's where a politically astute negotiator differs from the average one.

David Carpenter, whom I introduced previously, knows when he isn't the person to do the negotiating. "I learned to notice when my chemistry isn't right and when I need to bring in someone else to handle it or help out." Most people don't do this, Carpenter says. They make the mistake of staying in the negotiation or sale even when they're the wrong person to be working with a particular client.

There are different styles of negotiation. Sometimes different styles don't mesh. USC Professor Emeritus Alan Rowe and I have developed an assessment tool for identifying negotiation style predilections. Like the LSI, which identifies preferences among four leadership styles, the NSI identifies preferences among four negotiation styles: Achiever, Analytical, Motivator, and Mediator.

NEGOTIATION STYLE – 1.3

To score the instrument, use the same procedure as that of the LSI. Put an 8 next to the response *Most* like you, a 4 for the response *Moderately* like you, a 2 for the response a *Little* like you, and a 1 for the response *Least* like you. Then add down each column. The four numbers should equal 300. YOU MUST ANSWER ALL THE QUESTIONS. THERE ARE NO RIGHT OR WRONG ANSWERS. The answers reflect how you see yourself so respond with what comes first to your mind.

1. When I negotiate, I	focus on my objectives 1	explore workable solutions 4	try to understand their thinking 2	try to avoid arguments 8
2. I explain my ideas best by	being forceful 1	presenting my ideas logically 8	explaining the implication 2	relating my points to theirs 4
3. When I am confronted, I	react strongly to what is said 1	explain my position with facts 8	look for a common ground 4	give in reluctantly 2
4. I describe my expectations	objectively 1	in complete detail 2	enthusiastically 4	amicably 8
5. I get my best deals when I	don't make any concessions 1	utilize my leverage 8	find creative solutions 4	am willing to meet them half way 2
6. My objective in negotiation is to	achieve my goal 1	convince others to accept my position 8	find the best solution for all 4	look for an acceptable solution 2
7. The way to win an argument is to	be self-confident 1	be logical 4	have novel ideas 2	look for consensus 8
8. I prefer information that	is specific and understandable 8	is complete and persuasive 4	shows a number of options 2	helps to achieve rapport 1
9. When I'm not sure what to do, I	take direct action 1	search for possible solutions 4	rely on my intuition 2	seek advice from others 8
10. I dislike	long debates 1	incomplete information 2	highly technical material 8	having arguments 4
11. If I've been rejected, I	persist in my point of view 8	rethink my position 2	relate my ideas to theirs 1	try to salvage the relationship 4
12. If timing is important, I	press for a quick decision 2	rely on critical facts 4	propose a compromise 8	hope to postpone the inevitable 1

13. When I am questioned, I	answer emphatically *1*	rely on data for my position *8*	respond with a broad question *2*	look at how it affects me *4*
14. I prefer situations where	I am in control *1*	I can utilize my logical ability *2*	I can explore new opportunities *4*	people are considerate *8*
15. I negotiate best when	I use my experience *1*	a technical analysis is critical *4*	I can explore many alternatives *2*	I am in a win-win situation *8*
16. When I am the underdog, I	do not show any weakness *4*	prepare carefully *8*	try to change the situation *1*	match my needs with theirs *2*
17. When one is antagonistic, I	stand my ground *1*	reason things out carefully *2*	attempt to rise above the situation *8*	look for ways to reduce the tension *4*
18. If I'm in a losing situation, I	become more determined *1*	consider all my options *2*	look for ways to turn it around *8*	appeal to their sense of fairness *4*
19. To achieve mutual gain, I	show a workable solution *1*	clarify everyone's priorities *2*	suggest a mutually beneficial plan *8*	consider both sides of the issue *4*
20. In negotiating, it is important to	Know what each party wants *2*	clearly identify the agenda *8*	start by making a positive impression *1*	recognize that each party has needs *4*

Alan J. Rowe and Kathleen K. Reardon 12/29/97, rev. 3/27/98
(This form may not be reproduced without written permission)

39   94   77   90

Achievers (highest score in column one) usually go right to the heart of an issue, moving things along quickly. They have little patience for long-winded logic, and they want to win. *Analytical* (highest score in column two) negotiators provide a good deal of data and are inclined to walk people through their reasoning step by step. They speak in terms of priorities, and, if they make concessions, they tend to make them along these lines. *Motivators* (highest score in column three) pride themselves on finding clever, novel ways of reaching solutions. They also express enthusiasm in contagious fashion. Finally, *Mediators* (highest score in column four) like to help people find ways to agree. They are inclined to seek compromise or to accommodate so that things work out well for everyone. While these four style types are similar to the LSI style types described in chapter 4, most people have at least somewhat different leadership and negotiation style preferences.

As you can see, as with leadership, each style type is potentially in conflict with the other types. The Achiever, for example, could become very annoyed with an Analytical who provides too much data, with a Motivator who is a dreamer rather than a doer, or with a Mediator who seems to be looking for happy endings.

Often backup styles (second and sometimes third highest scores on the inventory) prove helpful in bridging communication gaps. An Achiever with a backup Analytical style could be patient with a strong Analytical type because he or she is familiar with that style.

When the styles are at odds, though, and backup styles don't mesh either, the mix isn't conducive to successful negotiation. To be an effective negotiator, you need to pick up on when you're unable to stretch to accommodate the style preferences of the other party. That's when you may need to fold up your tent and let someone else take over or give you a hand.

Elizabeth Daley, dean of the Cinema School and head of the Annenberg Center at USC, told me that she learned long ago that relying solely on your own skill is a good way to dead-end your career. "I learned from a friend that there is an important difference between people who do really well and those who only do moderately well in their careers. When confronted with a challenge, the ones who do really well ask themselves, 'Who can help me with this?' Those who only do moderately well ask themselves, 'What can I do about this?' " It's a subtle but important distinction.

Returning to the earlier scenario, Mike has already made some serious mistakes which his home office has noticed. That's why Ellen was sent along. But rather than focusing on the goal of the negotiation, she is focused on how each man is responding to her. And Gene is focused on what he sees as Mike's arrogance. They're all out to prove themselves. In approaching the negotiation, none of them is

questioning whether his or her primary style is suited to the negotiation at hand. They aren't wondering, based on first impressions,
whether their backup styles might help them stretch to communicate more effectively with the others. They're not demonstrating the
kind of sensitivity to differences that it takes to negotiate effectively.

They should be asking themselves how their style strengths
might prove useful at anticipated junctures in the upcoming negotiation. If Ellen knows, for example, that she is more Analytical than
Mike and that he is more of an Achiever, then she may be better
positioned than Mike to provide data to support their claims. Mike,
on the other hand, is better suited to creating a sense of urgency and
ushering the negotiation away from excessive discussions that could
take them away from reaching a workable solution.

Savvy negotiation requires this kind of questioning. Gene should be
assessing how he might have to stretch his style to get and keep Mike and
Ellen's interest and attention. In negotiation the goal is to achieve the best
outcome under the circumstances. If you don't assess the circumstances,
including style differences, your outcome is likely to be compromised.

Organize Your Thoughts into Primary Issues, Secondary Issues, and Clutter Issues

Colin Powell uses the KISS principle to guide his communication:
Keep it simple, stupid.[1] Too often people go into negotiation without knowing which goals are most important to them. Politically
savvy negotiators are organized; they keep things as simple as possible (unless ambiguity actually helps them reach their goals—even
then the ambiguity is contrived, not accidental).

It never pays to go into negotiations with just one plan. You need contingency plans too.[2] It's critical to establish and to organize strategies and options in terms of preference. Most important, you can't allow the discussion to get lost in minor issues if you're going to make a good impression and get what you're after. The best negotiators are very good at candidly answering this question: Am I getting bogged down in details that are taking me away from my main goal? In advance of negotiations, they ask themselves, "What issues do I want to avoid?" Then they apply the KISS principle, because they know that too much complexity leaves open many avenues down which the negotiation might meander to its demise.

Get Yourself a Good Opener

Since people often rush to judgment about each other and make quick, negative assumptions, it's important to get negotiations off to a strong start. In negotiation parlance, this is called a strong "opening stance." Sometimes this means beginning with an apology, to decrease expected animosity. At other times, it means making a firm statement about expectations so the other side knows you're serious.

More often than not, a good opening stance is a well-planned one. Richard Lewis, CEO of Accountants Overload, has a good saying that applies here: "It's better to be silent and be thought a fool than to speak and remove all doubt." In negotiation it's always better to think before you speak. Take the time to consider how what you say will influence the other party's reply and how that reply might limit your options.

Rather than starting by telling the other side your strongest argument or revealing your position, it's often a good idea to start with a question, although not just any question. The choice of question type should be strategic. Open-ended questions, for example, are ones that require more than a simple *yes* or *no* answer. "What would you like to achieve at this meeting?" and "What do you think of our plan?" are examples of open-ended questions. The best time to use these kinds of questions is when you need more information about how the other side is approaching the issue at hand. Another time might be when there's a good chance that they're angry with you and so you want to give them the opportunity to vent early in the negotiation.

To make the venting of anger work, you need to be careful not to react to any emotional outbursts or criticisms. Your response to such an occurrence might be: "I don't blame you for feeling as you do. There's been a considerable amount of misinformation prior to this meeting and some incidents that shouldn't have occurred. And that's why we're here today, to turn that situation around. Maybe you have some thoughts on how we might do that."

Openers set the stage. When the curtain goes up, a theater audience formulates an impression within seconds. Get it wrong and the performers spend the next few hours making up for a poor start. What separates the politically astute negotiator from the less advanced is sensitivity to those first few seconds and minutes. Assess early on what matters to the other party, demonstrate that you are also concerned about these matters and that you're there to work with him or her, and you'll be off on the right track in 95 percent of negotiations.

Become a Multitracker

The ability to observe on many levels is one of the least discussed yet most important negotiation skills. One reason why so few people do this well is that there's a tendency to think that negotiation is mostly about words. Even the most popular negotiation books focus on what you should say to get the upper hand or achieve accord where there's been dissension. The truth, however, is that a considerable amount of success in negotiation comes from reading cues that others miss, calculating their importance, and sometimes giving them greater credence than the spoken word.

There are few people who've achieved the secret handshake without honing the skill of *seeing what others disregard,* whether it's a slight tilt of the CEO's head at a meeting, a senior vice-president's glance at her watch, a rapid change of topic, or a momentary grimace. Whatever the subtle signal, the most savvy don't miss it. They think over their observations of subtle signals and decide whether they're meaningful. If the boss looks bored, they'll speak in a louder tone of voice, use direct eye contact and perhaps humor to shake him out of his malaise into interest and curiosity.

Should they notice a slight shake of their opponent's head, their response might be, "When I first heard this idea, I was skeptical, but another way to look at it is . . ." By recognizing the other person's skepticism, framing it as natural and even expected, and then leading him or her to another vantage point from which to view the questionable idea, a skillful negotiator can dispose of opposition before it has even been stated.

Find the Connections

The key to negotiation, like the key to persuading, is to understand where the other person is coming from. Ask yourself: "What's most important to my boss or client?" "What are his greatest concerns?"

"How do they connect to mine?" Go forward only after you've answered these questions.

One of the more sage pieces of advice given by the people I interviewed came from a foundation director speaking about difficult bosses: "One day you just have to face the fact that you work for these people. Once you do that, a lot of other things fall into place. You let them know if you disagree, you might even occasionally argue your position, but once they make up their minds, that's it. You find a way to do it." Of course, there are exceptions to this rule. If you're asked to do something against your moral principles, for example, you might not do their bidding. With that exception, what most politically sophisticated people do is find a way to do what their bosses want while also advancing one or more of their own goals. This means that it's your job to find a way to connect what you want to what they want. Those who go off mumbling to themselves about doing what they don't want to do usually haven't thought beyond the immediate request. They haven't stopped to consider how what is being asked of them might in some way, if handled right, be a positive step to advancement rather than an annoying diversion.

Perhaps this section should be called "How to Please the Boss and Yourself As Well" because that's what we're talking about here. Linking goals, whether to your boss or to a client, affords the negotiation of differences. It involves identifying how doing what he or she wants might give you what you want as well. Ellen Nichols, a Hartford-based insurance executive, does this all the time. "I go in prepared to compromise and then to compromise some more, but I also know what I really want to achieve in the transaction. At impasses, I'm ready to say, 'How should we work this out?' I always go in with alternatives and I try to get them to join in with a 'How about if we try this?' approach."

This is the preliminary step to effective linking. The more prepared you are in terms of having alternatives ready that keep your interests in mind while serving theirs, the more effective you'll be. Too often people go into negotiations wanting an outcome they're unlikely to get, and then they keep pushing for it long after it is futile. Nichols warns, "It's critical to remember that there is always a bigger picture out there and something you may not have understood in your preparations. You have to keep your eyes open for it. You don't want to be like an angry child. You have to know when to stop fighting for something."

Does this mean you allow yourself to lose occasionally? It does if you aren't able to find links between what you want and what the other party wants. Coy Baugh, vice-president and treasurer of PacifiCare Health Systems, remembers almost losing an important deal over the placement of a comma in the contract. The discussion became very heated to the point where Baugh suggested the general counsel take a walk around the block. Realizing that the comma debate could ruin everything, Baugh adhered to one of his own axioms: Being right is only marginally helpful. He cooled things down and let the other side have their say. They worked out an addendum explaining how to move the "blasted comma," and everyone agreed to sign the documents. By hearing the other side out, controlling his temper, and finding a way to link their mutual concerns, the negotiation succeeded.

Make Yourself and Your Ideas Memorable

We've established that the human brain declines to be overtaxed. But what we haven't discussed is how to get and keep attention. Astute negotiators know how to grab attention and focus it on themselves and their ideas. Since negotiation is what most of us do much of the day at work, this is a crucial skill. You're more likely to get noticed and considered for advancement if you make a positive, memorable impact when you speak.

Nancy Hayes, a former IBM executive and now CEO of the Starbright Foundation, believes men and women create verbal impact differently. "Every one of the guys wants to be the guy who says the thing that turns the meeting around." This is how men often make themselves memorable. "Women, on the other hand, wait and listen. They try to determine the position of each person because they want to achieve consensus."

Whichever approach you choose, don't overdo it. Done sparingly, both the turn-the-meeting-around and the integrator approaches can make an impact and also make headway in a negotiation. The choice depends to a large extent on the culture of the company or companies. Watch carefully to see what gets people noticed where you work. If it's within your style reach, give it a try.

Politically astute negotiators also know the importance of making a nonverbal impact. James Farley was one of the pillars of the Democratic Party in the days of FDR. He was elected a member of the New York State Assembly in the early 1920s, and over the next twenty years his stature in the Democratic Party increased. He organized Roosevelt's successful campaign for governor of New York and, as chairman of the Democratic National Committee, led FDR's campaign for president. Had Farley not been Irish Catholic at a time when the United States wasn't ready to elect one, he might have taken the nomination he received to run for president in 1940. With all this success, it might seem frivolous to think that Farley bothered himself about being remembered in a unique nonverbal way. But he did. He started using green ink. And since no one else did, it made him memorable. He once said, "It occurred to me that it would be wise to have some little distinguishing mark that would induce the receiver to remember me as an individual . . . Green ink did the trick so well that it was given the job permanently."[3]

It seems odd to think that some distinguishing trait or feature could turn the tide of your career, and maybe it can't. But it might help. There are so many people who daily cross the paths of those with the power to promote you that it's difficult to be on their radar screen if you don't have something that makes you stand out. Don Butler, president emeritus and board member of the Employers Group, told me that one of his identifying features is cuff links. They're from all over the world. Each set is unique. At the time we spoke, he was wearing 22-karat gold tigers with diamond eyes. "No one fails to notice them," he said. "Each set is a memorable conversation piece."

Congresswoman Bella Abzug made her mark as a feminist because of her ideas, but it was her hats that made her recognizable and memorable to the general public. When I rode around Dublin with her after attending the Global Forum for Women, she had on a large-brimmed, beige hat. No one could miss her. During our cab ride to see the scenery the hat stayed on, and when she emerged from the cab, there was no doubt who she was.

After you've considered ways to make yourself visibly memorable, it's important to consider how to do the same for your ideas. Once again, in the morass of chatter that we experience each day, it's difficult to have your ideas reach front-and-center if you don't know how to get them noticed.

One way to make an idea memorable is to tell a short story about an instance when a similar idea worked effectively. You might also draw an image on the board, or conjure up an analogy that helps demonstrate how your idea fits with the discussion at hand. These memory-jogging, idea-clarifying techniques can be very powerful. Imagine, for example, that a joint venture is in trouble. You want to save it. The other side is dubious. You rise from your chair and draw a tree leaning precariously over a precipice. You turn to the group and say, "Our joint venture is like this tree. Its future seems in jeopardy. A strong wind could send it over the cliff. But let's look closer." You approach the board and draw several squiggles under the tree. "Beneath the surface, where we haven't been looking today, our tree has strong roots. It has weathered a number of storms, and if we feed it today with what it needs to survive, those strong roots will keep us secure."

An image can indeed be worth a thousand words, and an astute negotiator knows this. To the extent that you present yourself and your ideas in memorable ways, you create conditions for effective negotiation and advance your chances of being remembered when the time comes to select someone for a high-level position.

And if this ability isn't important enough already, there is good reason to believe it will be even more important in the future. Rolf Jensen, futurist and director of the Copenhagen Institute for Futures Studies, says, "We are in the twilight of a society based on data. As information and intelligence become the domain of computers, society will place new value on the one human ability that can't be automated: emotion, imagination, myth, ritual . . ." He predicts that in the future, products, and that means people too, will sell on the art of storytelling and that companies will recruit and retain people "based on how they express their spirit."[4]

If Jensen is right, and I believe he is, it isn't going to be enough to provide dry data to support the promotion of an idea or the promotion of people. If there aren't stories, images, and even myths as part of the package, then they'll be overlooked for something more tantalizing, something far more memorable. You'll want that something to be you.

14.

Channeling Machiavelli

———————◼———————

Throughout the interviewing, researching, and writing of this book, I've been aware that much of what has been described here might be considered manipulative. That's not a comfortable place for me—a professor of negotiation and persuasion. I even began to feel a kind of uneasy sympathy for Machiavelli. After all, he wrote a book aimed at helping his prince win wars and ended up being remembered as the guru of "the ends justify the means."

In my less defensive moments, though, I realize that while we'd all like to think that we've gotten where we have and will get where we're going based on technical competence alone, that just isn't how it usually happens. For most people, achieving the secret handshake involves surpassing many other would-be winners, and you just don't do that on brainpower alone. In a way, that's what Machiavelli was trying to explain when he wrote *The Prince*.

It's important to point out, too, that the word "politics" has fallen into some disrepute, not because of what it means, but because of how it has been used. Politics involves going outside formal rules and channels to achieve desired ends, and sometimes that's exactly what people need to do in order to advance valuable perspectives. Politics is, like it or not, the way things get done in most organizations. And it's high time we started to train people in how it works.

Finally, I'd like to end this book with an observation. I've spent much of my career studying how other people manage theirs. The most successful people I've met look at their careers much like chapters in a book. They adopt what Charles Handy describes as a "portfolio" approach to life, composed of collections of different activities with different goals.[1] They look at the world in terms of options. If these people weren't doing what they're doing now, they'd be doing something at least as interesting. This gives them a sense of power over what happens to them that others often give away. It also allows them to experiment and grow. They can experiment with the strategies discussed in this book because they aren't worried that something they do might ruin everything.

It's in this spirit of experimentation that the advice in this book is offered. If you don't try some new ways, you'll likely not go far. As one chairman of the board interviewed for this book said of the common penchant to stick with old ways, "I learned some time back that something that worked before doesn't work again unless it works." Unwittingly applying the old to the new is a sure career stopper. Warren Bennis captured this perspective in an interview: "There's a saying: Minds, like parachutes, work better when they're open."[2] Referring to CEOs but applying to everyone in business, he added that those who are successful "have their eyebrows continuously raised in curiosity. They approach the world as, 'My God, I can still learn something.' "

The need for constant learning also applies to managing the political landscape of work. It's ever-changing. What constitutes power and influence at one point in time may be passé six months down the road. The most accomplished, most successful achievers of the secret handshake have their eyes open and their ears to a number of doors. They don't fall easily into the trap of believing the obvious. They aren't movers and shakers of the obvious sort, but subtle, observant, and responsive to change. None of them are masters of the universe, nor do they see themselves that way. Much of what they've achieved has been hard won. Tell them that politics is so intangible that it can never be mastered and they'll tell you to look closer. That's what they did. And that's what we've done in this book. The true players know, though, that the political landscape of business is constantly changing. That's why you won't catch them sitting on their hands content that they've made it. If they want to stay in the game, they need to be alert. As one of them told me, "Most people like me have a big ego. But most people don't realize that we're actually always checking things, seeking information, and asking ourselves, 'Is this the right way to go?'"

Those who've achieved the secret handshake have the satisfaction of knowing they've "made it." But having done so doesn't keep you on top. The inner circle is constantly shifting. You can be in it today and out of it tomorrow. True players know this, so they're never complacent. You'll find them looking ahead to new life chapters, meeting new and interesting people, happily turning the next pages of their portfolios, adeptly scanning the field anticipating their next move. For them, politics is the vehicle that makes the ride to the top possible. The twists, turns, climbs, and sudden drops are all part of an exhilarating trip to be taken again and again.

Notes

Introduction:
1. Tom Peters, "Just Say 'Yes!'" Paper presented at conference honoring Warren Bennis, Marina del Rey, CA, May 6, 2000.

Chapter Two:
1. Steven Kerr, "On the Folly of Rewarding A While Hoping for B," *Academy of Management Journal,* 1975, 769–783.
2. Henry Mintzberg, "The Organization as a Political Arena," *Journal of Management Studies,* Oxford, March 1985, Vol. 22, Issue 2, 152.
3. Harry Levinson, "Assinine Attitudes Toward Motivation," *Harvard Business Review,* January/February, 1973, 73–74.

Chapter Three:
1. Kathleen Reardon, Kevin Reardon, and Alan Rowe, "Leadership Style for the Five Stages of Radical Change," *Acquisition Review Quarterly* 5:2, 129–146. On the topic of various intellectual strengths, also see Howard Gardner, *Intelligence Reframed: Multiple Intelligences for the 21st Century* (New York: Basic Books, 1999).

Chapter Four:

1. *www.achievement.org/autodoc/page/sch0int1*

2. See *www.t-o.com/sportswire/baseball/BBO-BERRA STEINBRENNE.html*

3. Alan Rowe, Kathleen Reardon, and Warren Bennis, Leadership Style Inventory, instrument for assessing leadership style. Available for use with permission from the authors. Contact K. Reardon, University of Southern California, Marshall School of Business, Los Angeles, CA, 90089-0808.

4. Kathleen Reardon, Kevin Reardon, and Alan Rowe, "Leadership Style for the Five Stages of Radical Change," *Acquisition Review Quarterly* 5:2, 129–146.

5. George Anders, "Boss Talk: Taming the Out-of-Control In-Box—For Amazon.com's chief, the Secret is Two Days for Strolling and Surfing," *Wall Street Journal,* New York; February 4, 2000, pp. B1 and B4.

Chapter Five:

1. Michael Dobbs, "Double Identity," *New Yorker,* May 29, 1999, p. 53.

2. Daphne Merion, *New Yorker,* June 14, 1999, p. 78.

3. Judith Hennessee, *Betty Friedan: Her Life* (New York: Random House, 1999).

4. Betty Friedan, *Life So Far* (New York: Simon & Schuster, 2000).

5. *www.achievement.org,* p. 3 of 6, June 17, 1994, interview.

Chapter Six:

1. Erving Goffman, *The Presentation of Self in Everyday Life* (Garden City, NY: Doubleday, 1959).

2. Erving Goffman, *Relations in Public* (New York: Basic Books, 1971).

3. Ellen Langer, "Rethinking the Role of Thought in Social Interaction," in H. Harvey, W. Ickes, and R. Kidd, eds., *New Directions in Attribution Research,* vol. 2 (Hillsdale, NJ: Erlbaum, 1978), pp. 35–50.

4. Kathleen Reardon, *Persuasion in Practice* (Thousand Oaks, CA: Sage Publications, 1991).

5. Kathleen Reardon, *International Business Gift Customs* (Stanford, CA: Passepartout, 1987), and website *internationalgiftpage.com*

6. Gregory Bateson, Paul Watzlawick, Janet Beavin, and Donald Jackson, *Pragmatics of Human Communication: A Study of Interactional Patterns, Pathologies, and Paradoxes* (New York: Norton, 1967).

Chapter Seven:

1. Paul Watzlawick, Janet Beavin, and Donald Jackson, *Pragmatics of Human Communication: A Study of Interactional Patterns, Pathologies, and Paradoxes* (New York: Norton, 1967).
2. Richard Petty and John Cacioppo, "The Effects of Involvement on Responses to Argument Quantity and Quality: Central and Peripheral Routes to Persuasion," *Journal of Personality and Social Psychology* 46, 69–81. 1984.
3. Kathleen Reardon, *They Don't Get It, Do They? Closing the Communication Gap Between Women and Men* (New York: Little, Brown, 1995).
4. Frank Millar and Edna Rogers, "A Relational Approach to Interpersonal Communication," in Gerald R. Miller, ed., *Explorations in Interpersonal Communication* (Beverly Hills, CA: Sage Publications, 1976); Watzlawick, Beavin, and Jackson, *Pragmatics of Human Communication;* Gregory Bateson, *Steps to an Ecology of Mind: Collected Essays in Anthropology, Psychiatry, and Epistemology,* University of Chicago Press, 2000.
5. Reardon, *They Don't Get It, Do They?*
6. Klaus Krippendorf, "Undoing Power," *Critical Studies in Mass Communication* 12:2 (1995), 101–132.

Chapter Eight:

1. On May 6, 2000, a group of management experts from around the world gathered to honor Warren Bennis for his contributions to the study of leadership. The ideas shared at that conference had considerable relevance to the study of politics. Information about that conference can be obtained from the Leadership Institute at the Marshall School of Business, University of Southern California.
2. Mihaly Csikzentmihalyi, *Flow: The Psychology of Optimal Experience* (New York: Harper & Row, 1970).
3. Peter Frost, "Power, Politics, and Influence," in F. Jablin, L. Putnam, K. Roberts, and L. Porter, eds., *Handbook of Organizational Communication* (Newbury Park, CA: Sage, 1987), 228–263.
4. Margaret Mead, *Male and Female* (New York: William Morrow, Quill, 1975).
5. Edwin P. Hollander, "Conformity, Status, and Idiosyncrasy Credit," in *Psychological Review,* 65, 117–127, 1958.

Chapter Nine:

1. See Michel Foucault, *Power/Knowledge: Selected Interviews and Other Writings 1972–1977* (New York: Pantheon, 1980); Joanne Martin and Debra Meyerson, "Women and Power: Conformity, Resistance, and Disorganized Coaction," in R. Kramer and M. Neale, eds., *Power and Influence in Organizations* (Thousand Oaks, CA: Sage Publications, 1998), pp. 311–348.

2. Alan Sheridan, Michel Foucault, *The Will to Truth* (New York and London: Tavistock Publications, 1980).

3. Klaus Krippendorf, "Undoing Power," *Critical Studies in Mass Communication* 1995, 12:2, 101–132.

4. Robin Lakoff, *Talking Power* (New York: Basic Books, 1990), p.13.

5. Plato, "Apology," in Frank N. Magill, ed., *Masterpieces of World Philosophy* (New York: HarperCollins, 1990), pp. 33–41.

6. Rosabeth Moss Kanter, "Power Failure in Management Circuits," *Harvard Business Review,* July/August 1979, p. 65.

7. Stanley Deetz, *Democracy in an Age of Corporate Colonization* (New York: State University of New York Press, 1992), pp. 302–303.

8. Robert Slater, *Jack Welch and the GE Way* (New York: McGraw-Hill, 1999).

9. Karl Weick, *Sensemaking in Organizations* (Thousand Oaks, CA: Sage, 1995).

10. Linda Hill, "Power Dynamics in Organizations," Harvard Business School Press, note number 9-494-083, March 22, 1995.

Chapter Ten:

1. Jeffrey Pfeffer and Robert Sutton, "The Smart Talk Trap," *Harvard Business Review,* May/June, 1999, p. 136. Vol. 7(3)

2. B. Bass and R. Stogdill, *Handbook of Leadership* (New York: Free Press, 1981).

3. Charles Handy, *Understanding Organizations* (England: The Penguin Group, 1993 (fourth edition), p. 341.

4. Niccolò Machiavelli, *The Prince* (Chicago: The Great Books Foundation, 1955), pp. 59–63.

5. *The Portable Machiavelli,* ed. and trans. by Peter Bondanella and Mark Musa (New York: Penguin Books, 1979), p. 64.

6. Kenneth Blanchard, *The Heart of a Leader* (Tulsa, OK: Honor Books, 1999).

7. Philip Slater, speech, May 6, 2000, Marina del Rey, CA.

8. Thomas Davenport and Laurence Prusak, *Working Knowledge* (Boston: Harvard Business School Press, 1998).

9. John Seely Brown, speech, May 6, 2000, Marina del Rey, CA.

10. Ibid.

11. Sidney Harman, speech, May 6, 2000, Marina del Rey, CA.

12. Steve Kerr's books include coauthoring *The Boundaryless Organization* (Jossey-Bass, 1995) and editing *Ultimate Rewards* (Harvard Business School Press, 1997).

13. James O'Toole, speech, May 6, 2000, Marina del Rey, CA.

14. Jean Lipman-Blumen, speech, May 6, 2000, Marina del Rey, CA.

15. Frances Hesselbein, speech, May 6, 2000, Marina del Rey, CA.

Chapter Eleven:

1. Gary Heil, Warren Bennis, and Deborah Stephens, *Douglas McGregor, Revisited* (New York: John Wiley, 2000), p. 74.

2. "Mitchell Built Foundation of Trust for N. Ireland," *Los Angeles Times,* November 19, 1999, p. A16.

3. Anna Muoio, ills. By Alison Seiffer, "Bass Management Unit of One," *Fast Company,* April 1999, issue 23, p. 91.

4. My gratitude to Connie Noblet, for sharing with me "fluffing the dove" techniques which she has used in her work with the National Organization for Victims' Assistance (NOVA), endeavoring to educate politicians, police, and the general public regarding the needs of crime victims.

5. Jules B. Rotter, "Generalized Expectancies for Internal versus External Control of Reinforcement," *Psychological Monographs,* 1966, 80, 1.

6. Robert Bies and Thomas Tripp, "Two Faces of Powerlessness: Coping with Tyranny in Organizations," in R. Kramer and M. Neale, eds., *Power and Influence in Organizations* (Thousand Oaks, CA: Sage Publications, 1998), p. 213.

7. Carol Gilligan, *In a Different Voice* (Cambridge, MA: Harvard University Press, 1992); Kathleen Reardon, *They Don't Get It, Do They?* (New York: Little, Brown, 1995).

8. Karen Lillington, "Woman in Top Job Should Not Be a Big Deal," *The Irish Times,* 1999.

9. See Shelley Taylor, *Positive Illusions* (New York: Basic Books, 1989).

10. Lynn Miller, Linda Cooke, Jennifer Tsang, and Faith Morgan, "Should I

Brag? Nature and Impact of Positive and Boastful Disclosures for Women and Men," *Human Communication Research*, March 1992, pp. 364–399.

Chapter Twelve:
1. Chris Argyris, "Good Communication That Blocks Learning," *Harvard Business Review*, July/August, 1994, p. 80.
2. Kathleen Reardon, *Persuasion in Practice* (Thousand Oaks, CA: Sage Publications, 1991).
3. Michael Eisner, USC graduation keynote speech, May 13, 2000.
4. Ann Majchrzak, "Net Teams: It's Not Rocket Science," *Marshall Magazine*, Spring 2000, pp. 50–51.

Chapter Thirteen:
1. Colin Powell, speech for Outreach America Program at Sears Headquarters, Chicago, February 9, 1999.
2. Roger Fisher and William Ury, *Getting to Yes* (New York: Penguin Books, 1991).
3. "The Greatest Irish Americans," *Irish America*, November 1999, p. 57.
4. Cathy Olofson, "Dream Society," *Fast Company*, photographs by Colin Bell/CPI, issue 28, October 1999, p. 84.

Chapter Fourteen:
1. Charles Handy, *The Age of Paradox* (Cambridge, MA: Harvard University Press, 1994).
2. Warren Bennis, "Tomorrow's Leaders Will Combine Inspiration Introspection," *Los Angeles Times*, November 21, 1999, Part C2, Business, Times Mirror Company, 1999, p. 23.

Index

Chris Noblet

ABOUT THE AUTHOR

Kathleen Kelley Reardon, Ph.D., is a professor of management at the Marshall School of Business at USC, the author of several acclaimed business books, and a highly regarded consultant who has worked with IBM, Toyota, Xerox, AT&T, Siemens, and other leading corporations. She divides her time between Palos Verdes, California, and West Cork, Ireland